Copyright © 2023 John Williams
All Rights Reserved

ISBN: 9798851094972

Earth Plight

Global Warming: The Harsh Reality

John R Williams

About the Book:

Lake Mead near Hoover Dam: 20 June 2000 Photo: Private Collection

Global warming and climate change, while often used interchangeable, have different meanings. **Global warming** refers to increasing global **temperatures** believed by most climate scientists to be a result of human activities, primarily fossil-fuel burning that result in an increase in greenhouse gases in the Earth's atmosphere. **Climate change** refers to changes in the earth's **climate** that are the likely result of rising temperatures. Examples of these changes are rising sea levels, shrinking mountain glaciers, ice melt in the Artic and Antarctica, wind patterns, the number and severity of hurricanes, wildfires, droughts and floods. This book will explain how we got to this point in human history and what solutions are possible to reverse the harmful effects of global warming.

The **role** that **transports** (cars, trucks, etc.), **agriculture** and **power plants** play in global greenhouse gas emissions will be discussed along with possible remedies. The thoughts of leading scientists in the field of climate science will be revealed along with the thoughts of leading intellectuals. A 20-page pictorial of awe-inspiring photos of Glacier National Park taken by the author in 2011, occupy the center portion of the book. The **solution** and the **harsh reality** are also uncovered as the Earth plunges toward an **unknown future** and humanity's learning continues.

Mt. Jackson, Glacier Nation Park March 9, 2011 Photo: Private Collection

About the Author

*J*ohn R Williams has a bachelor's degree in math and physics from the University of Charleston, a master's degree in astrophysics from Florida State University, and has completed three years of doctoral study in nuclear physics at Auburn University. John is currently a retired professor of Physics and Astronomy at St. Petersburg College (SPC) in Clearwater, FL.

John has a long history of teaching and lecturing on the devastating effects of global warming. He has given seminars all over the Tampa Bay area about the consequences of continuing to pollute the atmosphere with CO_2 and other greenhouse gases. He has studied a multitude of possible solutions including those put forth by leading scientists and researchers. When the installation of solar panels rapidly expanded in the desert southwest, he advocated for their deployment on the SPC Clearwater campus, which was done successfully in 2011.

Professor John R. Williams receiving the Mentor of the Year Plaque from Robert P. Stasis, PE. FES Pinellas Chapter President 2011-2012.

Table of Contents

1. Humanity's Contribution to Global Warming	7
2. Transports (cars, trucks, planes, rail, etc.)	12
3. Power Plants and Faraday's Law	16
4. Nickola Tesla and the Evolution of AC	22
5. The Role of Agriculture	31
6. Possible Remedies	36
7. The Future of Food	45
8. The Evidence	54
9. Glacier National Park in Pictures	68
10. Thoughts of Scientist and Intellectuals	90
11. The Harsh Reality	107
12. Are There Solutions?	114

Acknowledgements

Many thanks to Dr. Robert Austin, Dr. Heyward Mathews and John Trever for their suggestions, comments and corrections.

Chapter 1
Humanity's Contribution to Global Warming

Humanity's contribution to global warming can be summed up by examining **three developments** that continue to add to our planet's temperature increases; **population gains, gasoline-powered transports** and **carbon-emitting power plants**. More efficient food production has allowed farmers to produce more food to feed an ever-growing population. Henry Ford introduced the assembly line and the inexpensive Model T Ford in the early 1900s, which allowed middle class Americans the ability to own and drive a gasoline-powered car. Nikola Tesla took the ideas of Michael Faraday to build the first hydroelectric power plant using the hydropower of Niagara Falls. The result was the production of alternating current (AC), which powers our modern civilization.

Keep in mind that **Global warming** refers to increases in **temperature** and **climate change** refers to changes in the **weather** that are often **the result of increasing global temperatures**. Drought, floods and wildfires are examples of climate change affecting humanity right now. The likely **cause** of global warming is the increase in greenhouse gases that are being released into the Earth's atmosphere at alarming rates.

[1] The majority of the public believe the media reports that claim the **main** greenhouse gases are carbon dioxide (CO_2), methane (CH_4) and nitrous oxide (N_2O). The reality is that because of its unique hydroxyl bond, the greenhouse gas **water vapor** accounts for **95%** of the earth's warming.

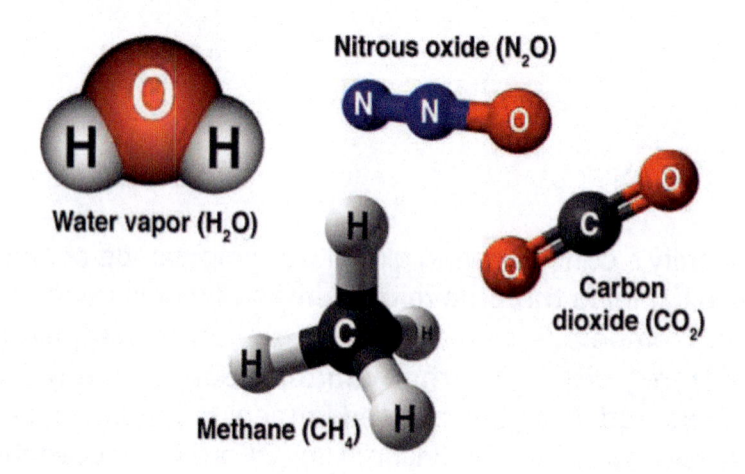

Water vapor (H_2O)

Nitrous oxide (N_2O)

Methane (CH_4)

Carbon dioxide (CO_2)

If water and water vapor were not present on earth, the planet would be a barren, lifeless rock. Since before dinosaurs roamed the earth, the amounts of water and water vapor have remained relatively constant. **This is often left out in discussions of global warming.** However, the **5%** of the greenhouse gases that do contribute to the **rapid increases** in global temperatures are caused by **human activities. Fluorinated** gases are especially destructive greenhouse gases, since they cause a thinning of the ozone layer. They include the chlorofluorocarbons (CFCs), which cause ozone layer depletion. They are commonly referred to as **Freon**. Even though these gases are emitted in small quantities, the global warming potential (GWP) of fluorinated gases is roughly 1,000 times greater than CO_2.

Our Planet has a Fever!

How do greenhouse gases contribute to warming the planet?
When sunlight passes through the Earth's atmosphere it warms the Earth's surface. This heat is then radiated back toward space. Most of the outgoing heat is absorbed by greenhouse gases and re-emitted in all directions warming the surface of the Earth and the lower atmosphere. This raises the Earth's average temperature.

For the Scientist: A portion of the electromagnetic radiation emitted by the Sun passes through the atmosphere and warms the Earth. The vast majority of the radiation is absorbed by the ozone (O_3) layer in the upper atmosphere and does not reach the Earth's surface. The harmful wavelengths that the ozone layer absorbs include gamma rays, x-rays and some ultraviolet radiation. The visible wavelengths pass freely along with the warming infrared. Radiation that has reached the Earth's surface is reflected back into the atmosphere and is trapped by greenhouse gases and then re-emitted in all directions warming the Earth's surface and lower atmosphere. Therefore the Earth's average temperature increases. If water and water vapor remain relatively constant at (95%) of total greenhouse gases, **why is the other 5% so concerning?** The reason is that this 5% is constantly increasing due to human activities, which gradually increase evaporation and water vapor. This creates a positive feedback loop that results in more greenhouse gases, more water vapor, more rain and more warming. When we consider what is **causing** the Earth's temperature to rise, **water vapor is not the root cause.**

[2, 79] All living and breathing animals have a carbon footprint, but humans have a **particularly large one**. Humans do much more than just breath, eat and sleep. From driving cars, to using their cell phones, an increasing human population is producing greenhouse gases at a catastrophic rate. In **1950** the world population was approximately **2.5 billion**. In July, **2023**, the world population was over **8 billion** (an increase of **5.5** billion people in just 73 years). The increase in just one greenhouse gas (CO_2) is quite concerning, since CO_2 can remain in the atmosphere for hundreds to thousands of years. Just to cite one example, according to Antarctica ice core samples, the concentration of CO_2 in the Earth's atmosphere is much greater in 2023, than at any other time in history dating back 800,000 years.

[3] **What about the CFCs and other halocarbons?** These products are used in refrigeration and aerosol propellants and are causing a destruction of the ozone layer. The ozone layer is humanity's protective shield. These products include halocarbon refrigerants,

solvents, propellants and foam-blowing agents (CFCs, HCFCs and halons). They are often referred to as ozone-depleting substances (ODS). When the Earth's ozone layer thins, more of the harmful ultraviolet (UV) radiation falls onto the Earth's surface. Scientists believe that UV radiation is responsible for skin cancers, cataracts and a few cases of permanent blindness. There is hope that these ODS compounds can be reduced and progress is being made. The **Montreal Protocol,** enacted in 1987, is an international treaty led by the US and signed by 197 countries designed to phase out the production of these ozone depleting chemicals. The **Kigali Amendment** to the Montreal Protocol was added and agreed to in 2021, giving hope for further recovery of the ozone layer. The Kigali Amendment aims to phase down the production and use of HFCs.

Chapter 2
Transports (cars, trucks, planes, rail, etc.)

Many inventors and innovators have contributed to the development of combustion engines, but only one was able to mass-produce the iconic Model T and make it affordable to everyday people. That man was **Henry Ford.**

[4] In 2023, there were over 1.4 billion gasoline-powered cars in the world. **The majority are in China** and the numbers are rapidly increasing. Attempts to replace these gas-guzzling vehicles any time soon **with electric cars**, will have an uphill battle.

[5] **Transport** accounts for roughly **20%** of global CO_2 emissions and **road transport** (cars, trucks) account for roughly **15%**. If all cars

and trucks were turned into bicycles, we would still have the remaining **85%** to deal with. If every car and truck became electric, carbon emissions from cars and trucks would be zero, but emissions from other sources to **produce and charge** these vehicles would quickly negate any benefit. The source of the remaining 85% will be discussed in the next **two chapters** as our story unfolds.

The man behind the mass production of gasoline-powered cars was the American industrialist, business man and Ford Motor Company founder, **Henry Ford**.

Henry Ford
Created: 1 January 1919 Hartsook, photographer
Ⓢ Public Domain

[6] He was born on a farm in Springwells Township, MI in 1863 and was the oldest of five siblings. He finished only the **eighth grade** and **never attended** high school. Upon his mother's death, he was expected to take over the family farm, but he hated farm work and wrote. "I never had any particular love for the farm – it was the mother on the farm that I loved." In 1891, Ford became an employee of Edison Illuminating Company of Detroit. When he was promoted to chief engineer in 1893, he had the money to experiment with gasoline combustion engines. Encouraged by Thomas Edison and other investors, **Ford unveiled the Model T in 1908 with the steering wheel on the left.** He then created a huge wave of publicity about the car. At a cost of $825 (approx. $24,880 in 2022), the car was both cheap and easy to repair. Sales of the car soon sky-rocketed, and by 1918, half of all cars in the United States were Model Ts. Soon assembly lines were able to mass-produce the cars, which were all painted black due to their faster drying times. Ford defended the color choice saying, "Any customer can have a car painted any color that he wants so long as it is black." The final total production numbers for all Model Ts from 1908 to its final year of production in 1927 was 15,007,034. As a result of the tremendous success of the Model T, Ford became the richest man in the US, with a personal net worth of **$200 billion dollars** adjusted for inflation. When asked by a reporter to estimate his net worth, Ford replied, **"I don't know and I don't care."**

[7] Ford believed in economic independence for the United States and was a big believer to paying workers **top wages** in order to keep employee turnover low and keep them happy. He believed in the global expansion of his company and felt that international trade and cooperation led to peace. By 1932, Ford was manufacturing one-third of the world's automobiles and had manufacturing facilities in 10 different countries. Ford, a prolific inventor, was awarded 161 US patents.

[8] Henry Ford had a passion for engineering and materials science and was proud of his company's R&D work and its adoption of vanadium steel alloys. Ford enjoyed many interests other than the Model T, which included plastics manufactured from soybeans. In 1942, Ford patented a car made almost entirely of this plastic. It was mounted on a welded frame, weighed 30% less than a steel car and was much stronger. It was fueled by grain alcohol (ethanol), instead of gasoline, but it never caught on with the public. He was also fascinated by engineered wood and felt that it could be much stronger than grown wood. He embarked on a futile search for a native source of rubber and formed the Edison Botanic Research Corporation which included Thomas Edison and Harvey Firestone as early investors. Ford published a book in 1914, detailing the **dangers of smoking**. It was titled The *Case Against the Little White Slaver*. It was aimed at the youth of America at a time when **smoking was pervasive** among the general public.

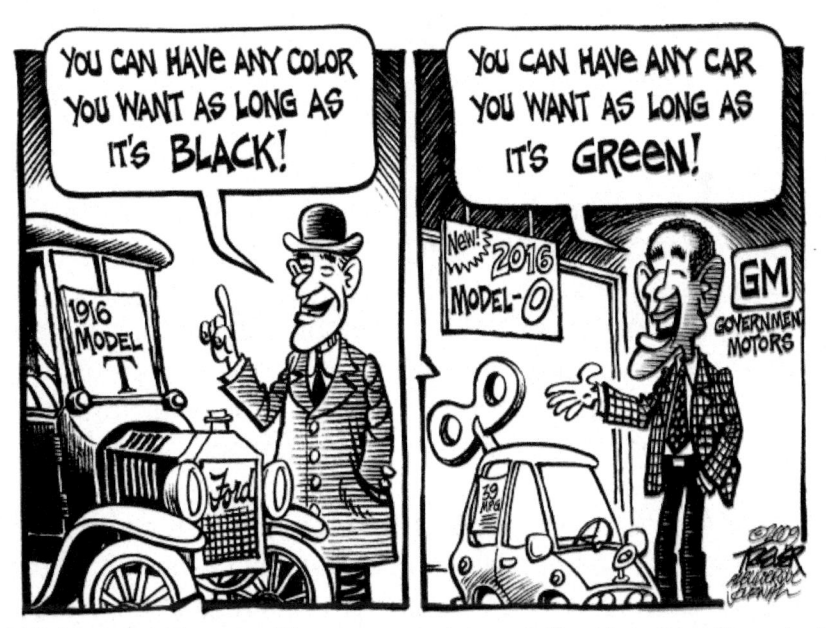

© 2009 by John Trever, *Albuquerque Journal*. Reprinted by Permission.

Chapter 3
Power Plants and Faraday's Law

$\mathcal{I}$n the previous two chapters, we have discussed humanity's greenhouse gas contribution to the Earth's atmosphere, specifically the role **cars and trucks** play by burning **gasoline**. Even though water vapor is the most abundant greenhouse gas at **95%,** CO_2 emissions from **road transport** create a vicious cycle of more greenhouse gases, more water vapor, more rain and more warming. This chapter discusses power plant carbon emissions.

[9] **About 64%** of the **world's electricity production** comes from burning **fossil fuels**. Ironically, one of the first power plants was The Robert Moses Niagara Power Plant which used the **hydro power** of Niagara Falls to produce electricity **without** burning fossil

fuels. However, the majority of power plants built in the last 70 years have burned coal, natural gas or oil to generate electricity. The industrial world, particularly the **United States** has done a credible job in **reducing** carbon emissions from power plants, but the rest of the world **has not**. Along with many developing economies, China continues to add coal-fired powered plants at an alarming rate. How do fossil fuels generate electricity? The answer to that question starts with the English scientist **Michael Faraday** and ends with Serbian inventor and engineer **Nicola Tesla**.

The **burning of coal** discharges a considerable amount of CO_2 into the Earth's atmosphere and contributes to the majority of the atmospheric buildup of harmful greenhouse gases. How then can a lump of coal be **magically transformed into electricity?** It can't, but the burning of coal can heat **water**, which can produce **steam** that can spin a steam **turbine.** The turbine then powers a **generator** to **produce alternating current (AC)** by **Faraday's principle of electromagnetic induction.**

[10] **The Law of Induction?** Faraday's Law of Induction can be stated mathematically (using calculus) by this equation.

$$\mathcal{E} = -\frac{d\Phi_B}{dt},$$

The equation can be interpreted as the emf produced in a single loop of wire is equal to the negative time rate of change of the magnetic flux. The magnetic flux is defined as

$$\Phi_B = \mathbf{B} \cdot \mathbf{S} = BS\cos\theta,$$

Where θ is the angle between the magnetic field vector **B** and the surface vector **S**.

[11] Born in 1791, Michael Faraday was an English scientist and experimenter, who discovered that a magnetic field was formed around a current-carrying wire. This discovery formed the foundation of electromagnetic field theory and led to his discovery of induction. Faraday surmised that since a current could produce a magnetic field, that a magnetic field should produce a current.

Portrait of Michael Faraday in 1842 by Thomas Philips
Ⓢ Public Domain
File: M Faraday Thomas Philips oil 1842.jpg
Created: 1842date QS: P571, +1842-00-00T00:00:00Z/9

In an effort to demonstrate this concept of induction, Faraday inserted a bar magnet into a solenoid (a coil of wire usually in cylindrical form) and was **puzzled** when a current was **not detected** in the solenoid. It was only when he moved the magnet **in and out** of the solenoid did he find evidence of an alternating current. Thus the concept of electromagnetic induction was discovered. Since Faraday only had a 6th grade education, it was left to James Clerk Maxwell to state it mathematically. Maxwell named it Faraday's Law and it ultimately became one of the four Maxwell equations. [12] These **four integral equations** form the theoretical basis for describing **classical electromagnetism**.

For the scientist:

$\oint E \cdot dA = Q/\varepsilon_0$ (Gauss's Law)

$\oint B \cdot dA = 0$ (Magnetic Fields – monopoles)

$\oint E \cdot dl = -d\Phi_B/dt$ (Faraday's Law)

$\oint B \cdot dl = \mu_0 I + \mu_0 \varepsilon_0 \, d\Phi_E/dt$, (Ampere's Law)

    E = Electric Field

    B = Magnetic Field

    A = Area of open or closed surface

    Q = Charge enclosed by surface area A

    $d\Phi_B/dt$ = time rate of change of magnetic flux

    $d\Phi_E/dt$ = time rate of change of electric flux

    μ_0 = permeability of free space (vacuum)

    ε_0 = permittivity of free space (vacuum)

[13] **James Clerk Maxwell** was a Scottish mathematician and scientist born in 1831 to well-to-do parents. James was an inquisitive youngster and an outstanding student at both the University of Edinburgh and Cambridge University. Maxwell's contributions to the fields of electricity and magnetism are considered by scientific scholars to be of the same importance as the contributions of **Albert Einstein** (Modern Physics) and **Sir Isaac Newton** (Classical Mechanics). Sadly, Maxwell died at an early age (48) of abdominal cancer. His mother had died of the same cancer at the same age.

The contributions of Maxwell, Einstein and Newton cannot be understated in the development of Physics, but without the efforts of **Michael Faraday** there would be no modern economy. Once Faraday found that a magnet could be moved through a coil carrying an electric current, his discovery paved the way for electric motors that operate in fans, vacuum cleaners, washing machines, electric cars and many other modern-day conveniences. After many unsuccessful attempts looking for the inverse (a magnet causing an electric current), Faraday, by accident discovered that a **moving magnet** inside a solenoid would cause a current to flow in the wire. This discovery led to the creation of the dynamo, or inverse motor, where a conducting wire moving in a fixed magnetic field would produce electric current. This same concept of electromagnetic induction in used in modern power plants today to produce alternating current (AC) or **electricity.** The telegraph, telephone and cell phones are all based on Faraday's induction law. If there were no Faraday, there would be no computers and no use of the binary system in electronic chips. Faraday took his work seriously and felt that conclusions drawn from data need to be supported by experimental certainty. The following quotes of Michael Faraday should give the reader some insight into the thinking of this giant of science.

"A man who is certain he is right is almost sure to be wrong."

"He is the wisest philosopher who holds his theory with some doubt."

"I have more confidence in the one man who works mentally and bodily at a matter than in the six who merely talk about it."

"Nothing is too wonderful to be true, if it be consistent with the laws of nature."

Chapter 4
Nickola Tesla and the evolution of AC

*O*ur modern civilization is powered primarily by electricity in the form of alternating current (AC) and the individual most responsible for its development and adoption is the Serbian inventor and innovator **Nickola Tesla**. AC induction motors are used in both the Tesla Model S and the Model X vehicles and DC motors are used in the Tesla Model 3 and Model Y. There are advantages to each motor. **AC motors** are less expensive, easier to work on and grip the highway better. **DC motors** last longer, are low maintenance and more efficient. However, the **evolution of electricity production (AC)** in power plants is where Nickola Tesla made his greatest contribution to modern civilization. The subsequent world-wide adoption of this means of producing and distributing AC has resulted in massive increases of CO_2 in our atmosphere caused by burning fossil fuels. Tesla immigrated to the United States and worked for Thomas Edison before striking out on his own. Edison, who had only a 6th grade education, was disliked by Tesla and he was not impressed with Edison's inventions or his work in electric power generation.

[14] Nickola Tesla was born in Serbia in 1856. His mother and father were both Eastern Orthodox priests. He was the fourth of five children and became interested in electricity after demonstrations by his high school physics teacher. He was an excellent student and could do integral calculus operations in his head. He was so proficient at performing these calculations, that some of his teachers thought he might be cheating. He finished high school with a sterling academic record, graduating in 1873 at the age of 17. Soon thereafter, he developed a **serious case of cholera** and was bed-ridden for nine months and close to death. His father, who had wanted young Nickola to become a priest, promised him that if he recovered, he would send him to the country's best engineering school. Nickola later claimed that the works of Mark Twain and his father's promise helped him recover from his illness. Two years later he enrolled with a scholarship in the Imperial-Royal Technical College located in Graz, Syria. Initially, he **excelled in his studies** and his father received a letter of commendation from the college dean. In the letter, the dean stated, "Your son is a star of the first rank." During his first two years at the College, Tesla was fascinated by lectures about electricity and electric motors, but by the third year **he was failing and never graduated**. There was at least one biographer who claimed that he was expelled for gambling and womanizing. After leaving school, Tesla cut off all contact with his family and began working as a draftsman for the meager salary of 60 florins (about $33 dollars) per month. Eventually he was found by his father and was convinced to return

home and resume his studies. After the death of his father at age 60, Tesla did attend lectures in philosophy at Charles-Ferdinand University in Prague, located in the present-day Czech Republic.

A Photograph Image of Nickola Tesla (1856-1943) at age 34
ⓈPublic Domain
File: Tesla circa 1890.jpeg
Created: circa 1890 date QS:P,+1890-00-00T00:00:00Z/9,P1480,Q5727902

Tesla was a 6' 2" introvert who weighed about 140 pounds and remained that weight for most of his life. He was fluent in **eight languages**, which included Serbo-Croatian, English, Czech, German, French, Hungarian, Italian and Latin. He was also a gifted mathematician and physicist, even though he obtained no advanced degrees. He was widely read, could memorize complete books and possibly had a photographic memory. He was immaculate in his grooming, a stylish dresser and his daily activities were highly disciplined. Tesla never married and claimed his chastity was helpful in his pursuit of his scientific studies. His views on women were widely viewed as controversial and may have been influenced by the women's suffrage movement of the 1920's. He once said that he could never be good enough for a woman and considered women to be superior in every way. His opinion of women changed a few years later, when he claimed that women were losing their femininity by trying to outdo men and make themselves more dominant. In an interview with the Galveston Daily News on August 10, 1924 he proclaimed, "In place of the soft-voiced gentlewoman of my reverent worship, has come the woman who thinks that her chief success in life lies in making herself as much as possible like a man. The tendency of women to push aside man, supplanting the old spirit of cooperation with him in all the affairs of life, is very disappointing to me." Two years later, Tesla seemed to take his view one step further by proclaiming that in the future, humanity would be run by "Queen Bees". He believed that women would become the dominant sex in the future. Tesla was highly critical of overweight people and once fired a woman for being too heavy. He rarely slept and never for more than two hours a night. His daily exercise consisted of walking 8 to 10 miles per day and curling his toes 100 times on each foot. He claimed it stimulated his brain cells. Later in life, he became a vegetarian, subsisting primarily on milk, bread, honey and vegetable juices. Tesla died alone in his hotel room at age 86.

Tesla meets Thomas Edison. After immigrating to the United States in 1884, Tesla began working at the Edison Machine Works in NYC. Tesla recalled the **change** he underwent going from cultured Europe to working in the slums of lower Manhattan, a **"painful surprise."** The first time Tesla met Edison was late at night while working on the damaged dynamos of the ocean liner SS Oregon. Edison thought at the time that "this [Tesla] is a damned good man". This admiration from Edison did not last long. Tesla quit working for Edison six months after he started, because of unpaid bonuses he felt he deserved. One account was that Tesla was promised a dubious $50,000 dollar bonus for redesigning and improving electric generators. Since Edison was stingy with his money, and the bonus would have been approximately $1.4 million in 2023 dollars, the amount was unlikely. When responding to Tesla about payment, some historians quote Edison as saying, "Tesla, you don't understand our American humor".

Thomas Alva Edison. Photographic print. Circa 1922
ⓢPublic Domain
File: Thomas Edison2.jpg
Created: circa 1922 date QS:P,+1922-00-00T00:00:00Z/9,P1480,Q5727902

[15] Thomas Edison was the youngest of seven children born in 1847. Edison contracted scarlet fever at age 12, and as a result was totally deaf in one ear and mostly deaf in the other. Untreated

middle ear infections may have also contributed to his loss of hearing. That did not stop Edison from being the most prolific inventor in American history, with over 1,000 patents. When he was 15, he saved the life of a three-year old from being hit by a runaway train. The son's father was so grateful that he trained Edison as a telegraph operator. At 19 years of age and with his telegraph experience, he moved to Louisville, KY where he worked the night shift at Western Union. He loved his job working at night, because it gave him time to spend on his two favorite hobbies, reading and experimenting. One night while experimenting with sulfuric acid, he spilled some acid on the floor and after seeping through floor, fell onto his boss's desk below. The next morning he was fired. Edison seemed to take his firing in stride and it wasn't long until he developed into a successful and ruthless businessman. He was responsible for developing 14 different companies including General Electric. Although Edison didn't actually invent the **incandescent** light bulb, he was responsible for a big improvement in its design. By 1888, this improvement and his development of direct current (DC) electricity production enabled him to build 121 power stations using DC. These power stations were financially successful, but soon competition from AC power plants became fierce. AC distribution at the time numbered 98 plants and was rapidly expanding. Edison had this to say about George Westinghouse, who was an early financial backer of Tesla and AC power plants. "Just as certain as death, Westinghouse will kill a customer within six months after he puts in a system of any size. He has got a new thing and it will require a great deal of experimenting to get it working practically." Publicly, Edison was never quoted as saying anything negative about Tesla, but AC and Westinghouse were a threat to his financially successful DC power plants.

But the real dispute between Edison and Tesla was a **clash of ideas**. It has been called the current wars or AC vs. DC. Tesla believed the future was AC. Edison believe the future was DC. With the aid of businessman, George Westinghouse, it was the genius of Tesla that made AC the power source of almost every home in North America and most homes in the rest of the world. The major advantages of AC are that it is easier to produce and **more efficient to transmit**. DC is easier **to store** and more practical for small devices, like car batteries, flashlights and cell phones. Electrical Power (P) can be expressed mathematically as,

$$P = IV, \text{ where}$$

I is the current and V is the voltage. Tesla who was well-versed in mathematics and calculus recognized that if you could increase (step up) the voltage, the current would decrease, thereby allowing the power produced to be transmitted long distances with smaller power losses (I^2R) than DC. The **R** in I^2R is the electrical resistance of the transmission wire. When the power reached its destination, the voltage could be reduced (stepped down) to power a home or business with AC. These adjustments in voltage could be achieved with transformers using the principle of induction, first proposed in the works of Faraday and Maxwell.

The clash of ideas became serious when Edison sensed that his profitable business of DC electricity production was being jeopardized by Westinghouse and Tesla's ideas of AC. Always the callous businessman, Edison tried everything he could to convince the public that AC was dangerous. He resorted to electrocuting stray dogs and cats in the streets of NYC with AC. He even tried to unsuccessfully electrocute an elephant. The public outcry over these outlandish demonstrations was fierce and the public began to turn against him. A major turning point came in 1893, when

Westinghouse won a bidding war with Edison to light Chicago's Columbian Exhibition for ½ million dollars. Edison's bid was twice that amount, so the lighting contract went to Westinghouse and Tesla. Edison's idea to supply low voltage electric current to America's households was flawed from the beginning, because low voltage DC current could not be transported over long distances without considerable power losses.

Edison did however have his successes. He was responsible for developing the **phonograph**, **motion pictures** and the **quadruplex telegraph** (allowed four separate signals to be transmitted and received on a single wire). Edison was twice married and had a total of six children (three from each marriage).

Mina Miller Edison, Thomas Edison 2nd wife in 1906
Ⓢ Public Domain
File: Mina Edison 1906.jpg
Created: 1 January 1906

When Edison died in 1931, The *New York Times* carried a largely laudatory obituary of his life and achievements. Tesla however, made this disrespectful quote in the Times' article. "His method was inefficient in the extreme, for an immense ground had to be covered to get anything at all unless blind chance intervened and, at first, I was almost a sorry witness of his doings, knowing that just a little theory and calculation would have saved him 90% of the labor…He had a veritable contempt for book learning and mathematical knowledge, trusting himself entirely to his inventor's instinct and practical American sense."

Chapter 5
The Role of Agriculture

Regardless of what they eat, humans and animals are 24-hour a day emitters of carbon dioxide and methane. In order to feed this growing number of humans and animals, agriculture has been forced to become more efficient at producing food and in the process has become a significant carbon emitter. It is estimated that food production adds approximately **20%** globally to the total amount of greenhouse gases produced by human activities. Considering that there is only a limited amount of farm land available on Earth, more efficient methods of farming are needed to feed an ever-increasing human population. For thousands of years, once land had become nutritionally depleted, allowing it to fallow was the only means of restoration. Allowing good farm land to go unused was an inefficiency that needed a remedy.

[16] It was the German chemist Fritz Haber who developed the remedy. Born into a well-to-do Jewish family in 1868, Haber won the Noble Prize in Chemistry in 1918 for perfecting the Haber-Bosch process. This method allowed for the large scale synthesis of fertilizers, which are used in nearly 2/3 of global food production. The key chemical in the Haber-Bosch process is ammonia, which is formed from hydrogen and nitrogen subjected to extreme pressure and temperature. Haber's discovery was founded on Le Chatelier's Principle, which states that when a system is in dynamic equilibrium and the conditions are changed, the system will try to minimize the change. Partnering with German Carl Bosch, a fellow chemist and engineer, they were able to produce industrial scale quantities of ammonia, a key ingredient in the manufacturing of nitrogen-rich fertilizers, which created greater agricultural yields and prevented billions of people from starving to death. **However, over fertilizing has led to the toxic release of N_2O, a potent greenhouse gas.**

Chemist Fritz Haber
Ⓢ Public Domain
File: Fritz Haber.png
Created: published in 1919 in Sweden in Les Prix Nobel 1918 (p 120)

Haber's parents were first cousins, who married in spite of major opposition from their families. Haber's mother Paula had a difficult pregnancy and died three weeks after Fritz was born. Fritz's father, Siegfried, remarried six years later and had three girls with his second wife Hedwig. Haber became close to his stepmother and his three half-sisters. Because of Haber's work in producing industrial scale ammonia, the world's annual production of synthetic nitrogen fertilizer is currently 100 million tons and is the food base for half of the world's population. In Haber's 1918 Nobel Prize acceptance speech, he said this about nitrogen's future role in agriculture. "Nitrogen bacteria teach us that nature, with her sophisticated forms of the chemistry of living, still understands and utilizes methods which we do not as yet know how to imitate." During World War I (WWI), Haber and many other chemists played a major role in developing chemical weapons, particularly chlorine gas for use in trench warfare. In the Second Battle of Ypres, Haber directed the use of chlorine gas against the Allied forces resulting in thousands of gruesome deaths. He is widely recognized as the "father of chemical warfare". In the lead up to WWII, Haber received extensive and well-deserved condemnation from Albert Einstein and other leading scientists for his role in chemical warfare.

Fritz Haber married Clara Immerwahr in 1901 and they had one child named Hermann. Clara was the daughter of a prominent chemist who owned a sugar factory. Clara was the first woman to earn a PhD in chemistry at the University of Breslau, located in present day Poland. She was a women's rights advocate, a pacifist, a perfectionist and highly intelligent. The marriage was contentious from the beginning and Clara eventually became severely depressed. After 13 years of marriage and following an argument with Haber, she committed suicide with his service revolver. However, she did not die immediately and was discovered by her 12 year old son Hermann, who had heard the shot. There are some reports that Haber's role in the use of chlorine gas in the Battle of Ypres was a factor in her depression. Her son Hermann, his wife and three daughters lived in France until 1941, and eventually emigrated the United States. Hermann's wife died soon after the war's end and Hermann committed suicide in 1946.

Clara Immerwahr
Ⓢ Public Domain
File: Clara Immerwahr.jpg
Created: circa 1890 date QS:P,+1890-00-00T00:00:00Z/9,P1480,Q5727902

Haber married a second time and had two children with his wife Charlotte. Again there were conflicts and they divorced after 10 years of marriage. In spite of Haber's conversion to Christianity, at least four of his extended family died in Nazi concentration camps.

[17] Haber's partner, **Carl Bosch**, who contributed to the Haber-Bosch process fared much better in his personal life. Carl was married once and had two children with his wife Else Schilbach. There were no known divorces or suicides in the family. Carl also won the Nobel Prize for Chemistry in 1931 for his contributions to

chemical high pressure methods that could be scaled for industrial use. He was an avid collector of insects, minerals and gems. His meteorite collection was loaned to Yale University and eventually purchased by the Smithsonian. He was also an amateur astronomer with his own private observatory. The asteroid 7414 Bosch was named in his honor. Carl regularly spoke out against anti-Semitism and many policies of Germany's Nazi party. The Institution of Chemical Engineers voted **Fritz Haber** and **Carl Bosch** the world's most **influential chemical engineers of all time.**

Chemist Carl Bosch
ⓈPublic Domain
File: Carl Bosch.jpg
Created: circa 1929 date QS:P,+1929-00-00T00:00:00Z/9,P1480,Q5727902

Chapter 6
Possible Remedies

The technical advances that have been made to satisfy the **wants** and **needs** of human beings have come at considerable cost to future generations. Humans **want** their cars and trucks. They **want** their homes powered by electricity, but they **need** food and water to live. These wants and needs have resulted in greenhouse gas emissions into the Earth's atmosphere that have resulted in global warming. The gas most responsible for this warming is **carbon dioxide**. Future generations will need to solve this global warming problem or face a perilous future. The **wants** of humanity can be mitigated, but not solved, with electric cars and trucks coupled with green power plants, but the **needs** of an ever-expanding population is proving to be more challenging. The efforts of global summits like the Paris Climate Accord and the Kyoto Protocol have revealed the difficulties of getting the global community on the same page. Currently, industrialized nations are bearing the brunt of reducing carbon emission, while developing countries like China and India have remained largely exempt. At this time in history, the reflections of a young Native American should be contemplated (heeded) as humanity is faced with a precarious future.

> "...And only time will tell if each generation is able to improve its life with the wisdoms of the generations before..."
>
> A. Hungry Wolf

Remedies to the planet's global warming problem need to be attacked from **two directions**. Carbon emissions have to be reduced and humans have to **clean up the mess** that they have already created.

What remedies are available to clean up our atmospheric mess? One excellent remedy for removing CO_2 from our atmosphere is a simple one. **PLANT MORE TREES!** Trees remove CO_2 in a natural way. They take in CO_2 from the atmosphere and release oxygen in a process called photosynthesis. **Deforestation** (cutting down trees) releases CO_2 and removes valuable absorbers of carbon dioxide. If the majority of humans would recognize the importance of tree planting and get started, this natural and efficient way of removing CO_2 from our atmosphere would go a long way in reducing excess carbon dioxide already in the sky. In addition to planting trees, removing dead trees and brush in our existing forests would reduce the severity of wildfires and add to the number of existing healthy forests, yielding more carbon dioxide absorbers. [18] Planting five (average lifetime 100 years) trees per year would offset one gas-guzzling car's yearly CO_2 emissions.

[19] Another promising solution for removing carbon dioxide from the **air is direct air capture (DAC)** which was first proposed in 1999 by Arizona State University (ASU) professor, Klaus Lackner. It is a process that removes CO_2 directly from air by using an aqueous alkaline solvent to extract carbon dioxide, which is then heated and compressed. The concentrated CO_2 can then be stored underground. Lackner also designed the prototype **mechanical tree** which shows great promise as a passive collector of CO_2. The mechanical tree needs no energy to collect CO_2, whereas the DAC requires large fans to suck in surrounding air. Direct Air Capture seems to be so promising that scores of companies have entered the DAC space.

[20] **Carbon Engineering** was founded in 2009 and is partially financed by Bill Gates and Murray Edwards. This company has partnered with a California Company **Greyrock** to convert a portion of the captured CO_2 into carbon-neutral synthetic fuels, including gasoline, diesel and jet fuel. The company uses a potassium hydroxide solution to scrub the carbon dioxide from captured air. Carbon Engineering's first plant became operational in 2015 and extracts approximately a tonne (mass of 1000 kilograms) of CO_2 every day.

[21] **Climeworks AG** is a Swiss company that as of September, 2021 operates the world's largest direct air capture facility, removing 4,000 tonnes of CO_2 annually. A larger plant called "Mammoth" is

scheduled for completion in 2024 and will remove 36,000 tonnes of CO_2 per year.

[22] **Global Thermostat** is headquartered in NYC and has an operational plant in Huntsville, AL. Amine-based sorbents bound to carbon sponges are used to remove CO_2 from the atmosphere. Global Thermostat claims to remove CO_2 at a cost of $120/tonne in its facility in Huntsville, making it one of the lowest-cost operations in the carbon capture space. Global Thermostat has partnered with Coca-Cola, who has plans to use the captured CO_2 for its carbonated beverages. Exxon also has plans for using the company's technology to start a DAC-to-fuel business.

[23] **Soletair Power** is a startup founded in 2016 and in based in Lappeenranta, Finland. The company absorbs carbon dioxide from ventilation units inside buildings to improve air quality. According to one study, the company claims that the improved air increases cognitive function by 20%. Soletair Power uses the captured CO_2 to make carbon-neutral synthetic fuels and as raw material for industrial applications.

Other companies in the direct air capture industry:

Infinitree – uses an ion exchange sorbent material to remove CO_2 from air which is then used in greenhouse applications.
Skytree – startup in Netherlands
UK Carbon Capture and storage Research Centre
Center for Negative Carbon Emissions
Carbyon – a startup in Eindhoven, Netherlands
Terrafixing – a startup in Ottawa, Canada
Carbfix – a Swiss startup with operations in Iceland
Energy Impact Center – a research institute that promotes the use of nuclear energy to power DAC technologies

Because of the many uses for carbon dioxide, society must recognize that carbon dioxide itself is not the "bad guy". It's only when there's an overabundance of CO_2 in the Earth's atmosphere, that the gas creates a bad result (global warming). Also remember that when we consume plants, we are eating a necessary component of photosynthesis (carbon dioxide). Other applications of DAC include carbon-neutral fuels, fertilizers, carbonated beverages, enhanced oil recovery, carbon sequestration, concrete strength improvement, carbon-neutral concrete, increasing yields of algae farms and air enrichment in greenhouses. The below chart are projections based on International Energy Agency (IEA) statistics as of September 21, 2022.

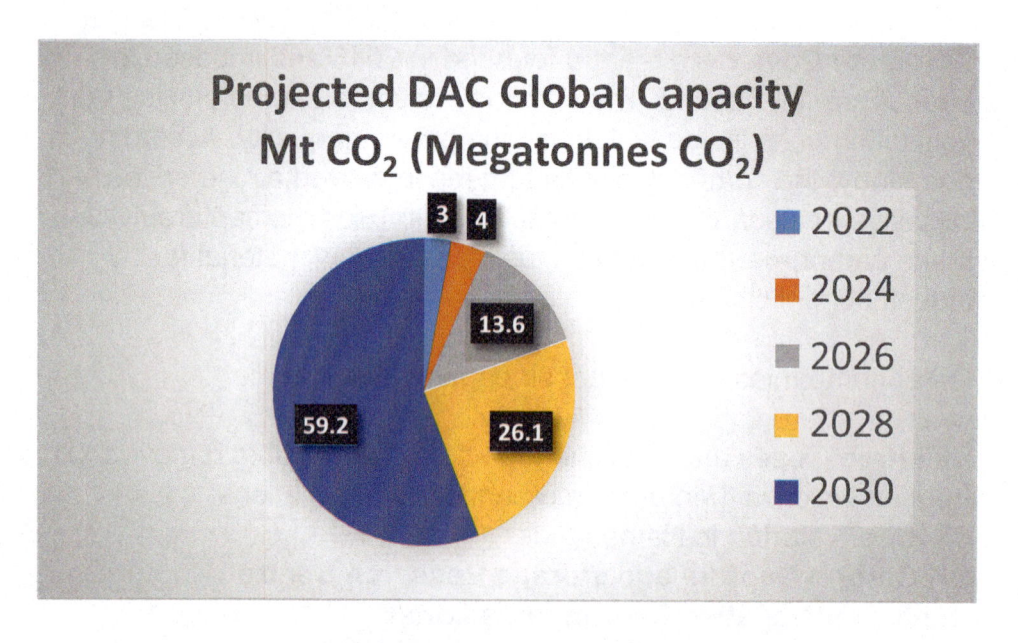

Projected DAC Global Capacity Mt CO_2 (Megatonnes CO_2)

- 2022: 3
- 2024: 4
- 2026: 13.6
- 2028: 26.1
- 2030: 59.2

Planned Projects (IEA)
Created: Pie Chart, J Williams October 14, 2022

To put the progress of DAC in perspective, the IEA reported that total global **CO_2 emissions were 36.1 Gegatonnes (Gt) in 2021** and should increase slightly in 2022. Since one Gt of CO_2 = 1,000 megatonnes (Mt) of CO_2, it should be clear from the previous pie chart that more help is needed and fortunately, more DAC help is on the way in the form of Mechanical Trees.

[24] **Carbon Collect's** Mechanical Tree™ technology is Gt capable, and consists of trees 10 meters (32.8 ft) high, which use absorbent tiles to absorb CO_2, using no energy in the process. Ten years of research and development has shown these mechanical trees to be a thousand times more efficient than natural trees for removing CO_2. The Ireland based company, Carbon Collect, refers to their proprietary technology as passive direct air capture (PDAC). The company claims that this technology is easily scalable and can remove up to one Gt of CO_2 per year. This amounts to about 3% of annual global CO_2 emissions.

[25] Seventy percent of the Earth's surface is **water** and it provides a vital carbon sink and a natural way of removing CO_2 from the atmosphere. Oceans and lakes soak up roughly 30% of the anthropogenic (human-induced) CO_2 emissions that are released into the atmosphere. When CO_2 and water (H_2O) react to form bicarbonate and hydrogen ions, our ocean and fresh water systems become more and more acidic. This is damaging to aquatic ecosystems, particularly our coral reefs. Not only can the bicarbonate ions later go back into the air as CO_2, the ocean's coral and mollusks cannot easily make their hard calcium carbonate shells and skeletons. Because this natural carbon sink is rapidly becoming saturated and increasingly more acidic, a method of CO_2 removal is needed. There are several direct ocean capture (DOC) technologies that are currently being explored that will accomplish an energy-efficient, low-cost, scalable CO_2 capture.

California Institute of Technology (CIT) is developing an offshore, stand-alone technology for efficient CO_2 removal from ocean water. Their primary objectives are twofold. First, a high operating current density and a low power electrodialyzer stack needs to be developed and demonstrated. Second, a membrane contactor that can facilitate a rapid removal of CO_2 from ocean water needs to be enhanced. These innovations show great promise in reducing capital and associated system costs. At a projected removal price of < $100/tonne, this process should have the capability to remove more than several Gts of CO_2 per year.

The **University of North Dakota Energy & Environmental Research Center** has plans to soften ocean water by hydrolytic softening in a low-cost process for CO_2 removal. This method is similar to the process used in water treatment facilities. The difference is that instead of the consumptive use of lime (CaO) to soften the water, calcium carbonate ($CaCO_3$) is decomposed which releases CO_2 and then regenerates the lime for continued cycles of carbon removal. Hydrolytic softening has been shown to greatly reduce energy input cost compared to other CO_2 removal technologies.

Massachusetts Institute of Technology is using electrochemical modulation of a protein gradient to remove CO_2 from ocean water. The method does not require expensive membranes or chemical additives and could easily be deployed on platforms or cargo ships.

More people, **more** cars, **more** electricity, **more** housing and **fewer** trees have created the global-warming predicament that currently exists on our precious life-giving planet. While cars and electricity can be considered **wants**, food and shelter for an expanding population are **needs**. At the present time, there appears to be no limit to the **wants** of humanity. Humans **want** their cell phones, cars, electrical appliances and central heat and air for their homes. In order to supply humanity's **need for shelter**, there are several excellent options for synthetic building materials that are carbon neutral, but the current options for carbon-neutral food production are limited. However, there are some interesting ideas that are currently under development that show great promise in increasing food production while limiting CO_2 emissions. These will be analyzed in the next chapter.

What about the nuclear option? The failures of Three Mile Island, Chernobyl and Fukushima power plants have created an uneasiness in the minds of the general public concerning the safety of nuclear power plants. However, the reality is that recently-built nuclear power plants are **extremely safe**. The current plants are fission plants and are carbon-emission free and a reliable source of electrical power. To produce AC, a reactor is required to control nuclear fission (a process where atoms spilt and release heat). Reactors use an isotope of uranium processed into small ceramic pellets, which are packed together in sealed metal tubes called fuel rods. A reactor may have several hundred fuel rods depending on the power being generated. The reactor is then immersed in water, which is then heated to produce steam. The steam then spins a turbine to produce carbon-free electricity. As of January 2023, there were 60 commercially operating nuclear power plants in the United States containing 98 reactors which are producing about 20% of the country's electricity. Globally, there were 400+ reactors producing roughly 10% of the world's electricity. Although there are no carbon emissions associated with nuclear power plant operation, there is nuclear waste produced and carbon emissions created in uranium procurement. In addition, the Earth has a limited supply of uranium.

Do controlled fusion reactors have a future? A December 14, 2022 article in the *Wall Street Journal,* reported that controlled fusion reactors do indeed have a future in electricity production. The US Department of Energy (DOE) announced a historic breakthrough in efforts to generate heat with a controlled **fusion** reaction. On December 5th, 2022, the Lawrence Livermore National Laboratory research facility in Livermore, CA achieved a first-ever controlled fusion reaction that produced more energy than what was required to produce it. Using the world's most powerful lasers, scientists were able to produce 3.15 megajoules (MJ) of fusion energy, compared with 2.05 MJ of energy required to trigger the reaction. **If this can be scaled** for use in power plants, it would mean no carbon emissions, no nuclear waste and a limitless supply of available hydrogen when producing AC electricity. The electricity produced could then power electric cars and trucks to make land transport carbon free.

Regardless of how humans treat the planet in the coming centuries, The **Earth will survive**, but civilization **may not.** If the Earth continues to warm, humanity will be forced to migrate toward the poles to escape not only the heat but devastating sea level rise. Countries and governments will be overrun with migrants trying to escape the harsh climates caused by global warming. Civilization's survival and the Earth's survival are two different things. The Earth will adjust, humans will adjust, but civilization **may not.**

Chapter 7
[26] The Future of Food

According to a September, 2021 **New Scientist** newsletter estimate, 37% of global greenhouse gas emissions are contributed by food production, with animal-based emissions producing twice as much as land-based ones. Because weather-related catastrophes are such a serious threat to global food production, changing the way food is produced and consumed is necessary to feed a world population that exceeds 8 billion. Human beings are creatures of habit and one of these habits is the foods they eat. **Three** foods comprise 60% of society's plant-based consumption. They are wheat, rice and maize (corn). The World Health Organization (WHO) reports that 29.3% or 2.3 billion people are food insecure. The United States Department of Agriculture

(USDA) reports that in the United States, 38 million people are food insecure, including 12 million children. Our food system plays a major role in greenhouse gas emissions, with transport and wasted food combining to create a wasteful system that needs to change. A 2019 report from the World Wildlife Fund (WWF) and the German food brand Knorr estimates that 75% of our global food supply come from 12 plant and five animal species. In addition, the United Nations (UN) claims that reducing meat consumption and adopting a more sustainable diet could reduce greenhouse emissions by 80% from the agriculture sector.

[27] The Knorr report entitled **Future Fifty Foods** recommends a variety of plants, grains, beans, fruits and leafy greens that should be more widely consumed, because they are not only nutritious, tasty and affordable, but less harmful to the environment than animal-based foods. General Electric (GE) reports that **3-D printed food** has the potential to offer consumers personalized nutrition for healthier diets and claims that by using multi-nozzled printers, any shape and texture can be consistently produced using cooked puree. This printed food method offers an option to feed the world's population in a nutritious and sustainable manner.

[28, 29] A San Francisco Bay area startup, **Upside Foods**, is able to use the cells from a **single chicken** to produce the same amount of meat as hundreds of thousands of traditionally-farmed chickens. The meat is then cultivated in a vat and grown from stem cells extracted from live chickens. The company is able to nourish these cells in a cultivator and form a cultured meat that is ready to pack in 2-3 weeks. The vat contains a serum that contains amino acids, sugars and other nutrients needed for cell growth. In the harvesting process, the chicken meat can be formed into shapes familiar to consumers, like chicken breasts. When produced in scale, the process will require a fraction of the land and water used in

conventional meat production. According to the Wall Street Journal, investors in the first round of funding included Bill Gates, Richard Branson, Cargill and Threshold. **Tyson Foods** and **Whole Foods** were also early investors and in April, 2022 an additional $400 million in funding was secured through investments made by the Abu Dhabi Growth Fund and Scottish fund manager Baillie Gifford. Upside Foods cleared a huge hurdle in November of 2022 when the US Food and Drug Administration (USFDA) announced that after a complete evaluation of Upside Food's chicken product, there were **no unresolved questions** about the product's **safety**. The CEO of Upside Foods, Uma Valeti, called the USFDA decision "the biggest moment in the history of our company". Although the meat product still needs the approval of the US Department of Agriculture (USDA) before it can be sold to consumers in the United States, the USFDA approval is a big step toward more sustainable meat products. As of this writing, Singapore is the only country that has approved the sale of cultivated meat products.

[30] **Other under-utilized foods that show great promise in improving sustainable food production** include **Ghee residue,** which is a by-product of ghee manufacturing. This residue can be used to make sweets and is produced in sizable quantities in India. This residue is a rich source of fat, protein and minerals and can be used in bakery items and certain dairy products. **Duckweed** is an aquatic green plant that can be found on the surface of lakes and ponds. It shows promise as a sustainable source of protein. It is a healthier and more affordable source of protein than animal meat. It can also reproduce using the vegetative method (see glossary). The vegetative method can increase plant yields over 50% per day. In order to mass-produce duckweed for low-income communities, an open-air system with direct sunlight with minimum fertilizing will be required. Another aquatic plant, which is both abundant and nutritious, is **Laver seaweed**. It is commonly used to wrap sushi

and can bring out the umami flavor in foods. In Wales it is used in bread. **Jellyfish** is a low-calorie, high-protein food eaten in Thailand, Malaysia, China and Japan. According to the Natural History Museum in London, there are about 25 edible species of jellyfish. They can be dehydrated or made into salads or sushi.

[31] **Nopales Cactus,** also called a prickly pear or cactus pear, is widely harvested in South America. It is extensively grown and harvested in Mexico and in the southwestern United States. The plant is high in antioxidants, vitamins and minerals and requires little water to cultivate. Many sources tout the medicinal benefits of this prickly pear. They include treating an enlarged prostate, lowering cholesterol and eliminating hangovers. The cactus is an excellent source of magnesium, calcium, vitamin C and manganese and can be found in a variety of Mexican cuisine. Nopales Cactus can be eaten raw or cooked and is used in soups, marmalades, stews and salads. **Amaranth,** originally grown in Argentina, is harvested in Asia and African for both its seeds and leaves. The seeds are rich in fiber and can be cooked like rice or popped like popcorn. The plant needs little water and the leaves can be eaten as a leafy green vegetable. The grain has a mild nutty taste and is great for soups, side dishes and risottos. The Aztecs referred to this ancient grain as the "food of immortality". **Buckwheat** is gluten-free and is a versatile grain with a nutty taste. It is often used as a cover crop and is a short-season grower that does well in cold climates. It is an excellent source of protein, dietary fiber and four B vitamins. Buckwheat is harvested and consumed primarily in Russia and China, but is harvested to a lesser extent in regions with limited growing seasons. In the parts of the United States, buckwheat pancakes are a popular breakfast item.

A variety of **Insects** are a great source of protein and are rich in fiber, minerals and vitamins. According to the Natural History

Museum they can be farmed, using fewer resources and emitting less greenhouse gases than livestock. They can also be ground up and added to both pet food and foods for human consumption.

Deep-fried insects being sold in Bangkok, Thailand

[32] **Fonio** is a drought-resistant ancient grain that has been grown in Africa for over 5,000 years. It is highly nutritious with a delicate nutty taste, is gluten-free and can be grown in sandy or acidic soil. Even though it is labor-intensive to harvest and process, fonio has the potential to boost nutrition, increase food security and support sustainable use of the land. Guinea produces about 75% of the world's production of fonio and readily grows in dry climates.

White fonio in Tambacounda Region of Senegal
Ⓢ Public Domain
File: SEN Village Chief Theodore.jpg
Created: 1 January 2006

Spelt is an ancient form of wheat that has been cultivated since 5000 BC in parts of Europe. It has a thick outer husk that offers protection from pests and disease. It can be easily grown without pesticides or fertilizers, but is **not** gluten-free. It has a pleasant, nutty flavor and can be used in place of rice. In Germany and Austria, it is commonly used as the main ingredient in breads and cakes. **Teff** is one of the earliest domesticated plants and is cultivated primarily in Ethiopia which grows about 90% of the world's teff. This ancient grain is grown both for its edible seeds and also for its straw, which can be used to feed cattle. The small (less than 1 mm in diameter) seeds are gluten-free and a staple crop in Ethiopia and Eritrea. Many consider teff responsible for the health and vigor of Ethiopian distance runners. **Khorasan Wheat** or Oriental wheat is an annual, self-fertilizing grass that is harvested for its grain. It looks similar to regular wheat but the grains are twice the size of modern wheat. Grown primarily in Europe, the wheat is nutritious and flavorful, but contains gluten. **Moringa** is a fast-growing, drought-resistant tree that can be used as a wind break to help soil erosion. The moringa leaves are highly nutritious and can be cooked and used as leafy-green vegetables. When ground into a powder, they add both flavor and nutrition to soups, sauces, smoothies, and teas. **Bambara groundnuts**, also known as Congo groundnut or Congo goober is a grain legume grown primarily in sub-Saharan Africa. It is extremely hardy and can be grown in drought conditions and low soil fertility. It is exceptionally high in protein and its seeds can be used as a food or beverage. **Wakame Seaweed** is one of a few plants that is a **great source** of omega 3 fatty acid (EPA). This acid is found mainly in certain fatty fish. It is widely used in Japan for soups, salads, stir-fries and side dishes. It is harvested year round in France, New Zealand, California and Argentina and can be grown without fertilizers and pesticides. Named for its hard outer shell, **black turtle beans** are popular in Southern Mexico and Latin America and commonly paired with white rice. In addition to being one of the best plant sources of protein, the bean is high in fiber and essential minerals making it highly nutritious. Multiple studies have demonstrated this black bean's value in lowering high blood pressure. **Edible packaging** shows great promise in reducing plastic pollution. Natural edible packaging, such as the skins of apples and grapes, are well-known, but less well-known is the process of using natural polymers extracted from plants to package food and drink. At a recent London marathon, runners were consuming edible drink pods instead of taking liquid nourishment from plastic bottles. Runners could then decide if they wanted to swallow the thin seaweed packaging or spit it out. The thin casing of these liquid-filled pods, called ooho, completely degrade in 4-6 weeks. Even edible tableware might someday replace plastic utensils, and if your preference is not to consume knives and forks, they are hyper biodegradable. Carol Culhane, a food scientist and a member of the Institute of Food Technologies, maintains that, "Edible packaging will find its place." As pollution threats from plastic intensifies, she feels this could soon happen.

Combining the thoughts of chapters 1-7, it is apparent that greenhouse gases emitted from human activities are contributing to **rising temperatures** on planet Earth. The vast majority of these gases are released by human activities in three sectors.

1. Electricity producing power plants
2. Transport activities (road, rail, air and marine)
3. Agriculture (crops, livestock)

Even though there are multiple remedies available to drastically reduce our carbon footprint, these remedies appear to be years in the future. Because these carbon-based greenhouse gases remain in our atmosphere for hundreds and in some cases thousands of years, future temperature increases are certain for the foreseeable future. Increased awareness of the severity of the challenge before us is crucial for humanity to act in a coordinated and effective way to reduce greenhouse emissions. Food choices, tree planting, electric vehicles, carbon capture and maintaining our existing forests will all help, but these common-sense solutions will require the participation of the world's entire population. Convincing the governments of **India** and **China** to stop building and operating coal-fired plants could make a colossal difference and would be a tremendous start toward a sustainable future for everyone. Climate scientists have provided a blueprint of what changes are needed. Now humanity just needs to follow the instructions.

[33] The prolific author Craig D. Lounsbrough, has written these words that can easily be applied to global warming. "Starting over is an acceptance of a past we can't change, an unrelenting conviction that the future can be different, and the stubborn wisdom to use the past to make the future what the past was not." Craig goes on to make an important addition by noting how **"... difficult it is to change a world that's in desperate need of changing, all the while denying the very change it needs."**

Chapter 8
The Evidence

*D*ubious evidence of the Earth's warming is readily available from friends, neighbors and the media. Older relatives will gladly relate how different the weather was in the "good ol days". Meteorologists will warn of hurricanes, tornados, floods and drought, but **reliable evidence** of global warming can involve some diligent research. In locations around the world, temperature and the weather may change from year to year (sometimes hotter, sometimes colder), but average global temperatures are changing in one direction only (**hotter**). There are many indicators of a warming Earth and here are a few. Global data supplied by the National Oceanic and Atmospheric Administration (NOAA) and the National Aeronautics and Space Administration (NASA) confirm that sea surface temperatures, land temperatures and air temperatures are rapidly increasing from year to year. Satellite data show a yearly decrease in the size and number of glaciers; a decrease in sea ice and rising sea levels. Along with increases in ocean heat content and humidity, the global scenario is clear. **Our planet has a fever.**

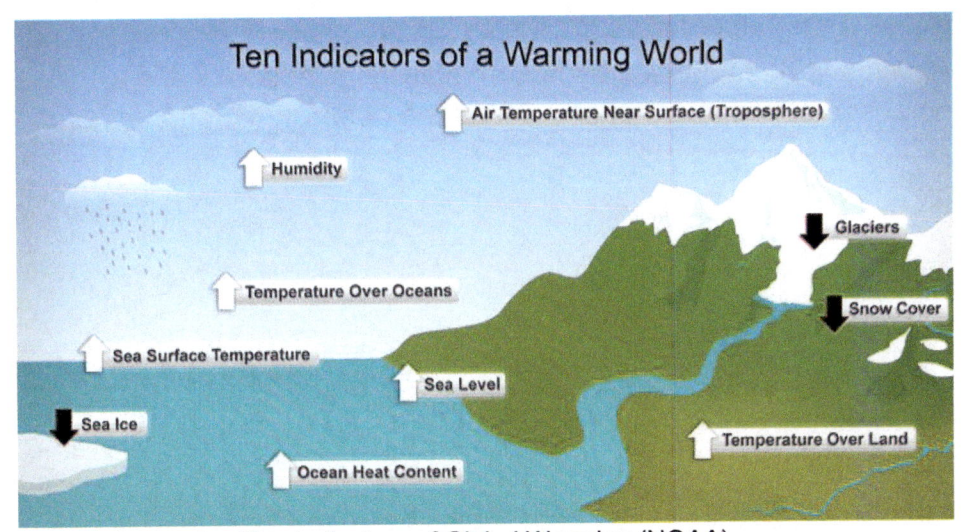

Ten Indicators of Global Warming (NOAA)
Ⓢ Public Domain
File: Diagram showing Ten Indicators of Global Warming
Created: 1 July 2010

[34] NOAA clearly outlines the seriousness of global warming by claiming that the first two decades of the 21st century were the warmest since global temperature records first began in the late 19th century. The data also shows that 2021 and 2022 global temperatures were among the warmest ever recorded. According to NOAA, the data shows an alarming trend. "When one reviews all the data, both from thermometers and paleoclimate temperature proxies, it becomes clear that the Earth has warmed significantly since the 19th century. Global warming has occurred. Multiple

paleoclimatic studies indicate that recent years are all the warmest on a global basis, of at least the last 2,000 years. The most recent paleoclimate data reinforce this conclusion, using longer records, new proxies, new statistical techniques, and a broader geographic distribution."

The conclusion that climate scientists have made is undeniable. The rapid global temperature increases observed during the last 50 years have been caused by human activity, specifically due to increased concentrations of greenhouse gases in the atmosphere.

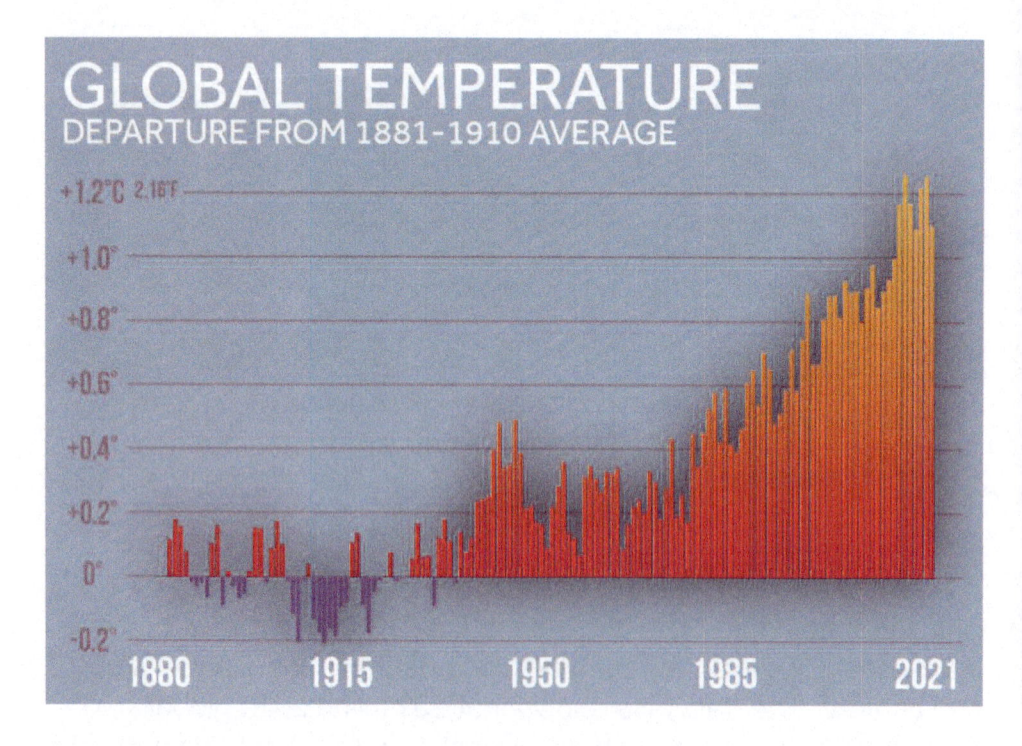

GLOBAL TEMPERATURE
DEPARTURE FROM 1881-1910 AVERAGE

Source NASA's Goddard Institute for Space Studies (GISS) & NOAA National Centers for Environmental Information (NCEI) global temperature anomalies averaged and adjusted to early industrial baseline (1881 – 1910).

Antarctic ice core data shows, this **rapid** increase is unprecedented and well outside the normal variation for at least the last 800,000 years. The peaks and valleys in the chart below are consistent with the glacial periods caused by change in the earth's position relative to the sun. These cycles were first postulated by Serbian scientist Milutin Milankovic and are responsible for the beginning and ending of glaciation periods (Ice Ages). Earth has experienced cold periods (ice ages) and warm periods (interglacial) on approximately 100,000 year cycles for at least the last million years. In the below chart the peaks represent warm periods and the valleys represent cold periods. These cycles correspond precisely with the Earth's orbital changes over a 100,000 year period. The Earth's **eccentricity** changes from 0.0034 (almost circular) to 0.055 every 100,000 years. The angle of the Earth's axis known as **obliquity** and the direction of the Earth's rotational axis known as **precession** play smaller roles in defining glacier periods. Even though a 10 to 15 Celsius temperature difference exists between glacial periods, those changes occurred **slowly** (over thousands of years) compared to the **rapid** warming today (over decades).

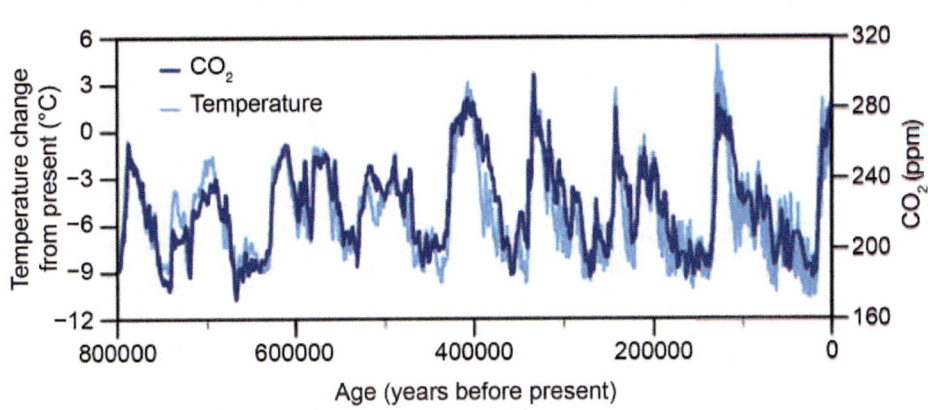

Temperature change (light blue) and CO_2 change (dark blue)
Measured from EPICA Dome C in Antarctica (Jouzel et all. 2007; Luthi 2008)

The deepest ice and the ice with the longest historical record is found in Antarctica. The method that climate scientists determine conditions thousands of years ago is from evidence found in Antarctic ice cores (proxies). More on this later in the chapter.

[35] What are the Milankovic cycles? Three Milankovic cycles play a key role in determining the Earth's long-term climate. A major factor is the 100,000 year cycle determined by the **eccentricity** of the earth's orbit (the distance variation from the Sun). Over time, the combined gravitational influences of Jupiter and Saturn cause the Earth's orbit to vary from nearly circular to slightly elliptical. Currently our orbit is nearly circular. The second cycle varies with the angle that the Earth's axis is tilted from the orbital plane called **obliquity**. The Earth's axis is currently tilted at 23.4° or halfway between the extremes of 22.1° and 24.5° and this cycles occurs every 41,000 years. The third cycle is known as **axial precession** (wobble). This cycle spans approximately 26,000 years. As the Earth rotates on its axis, it wobbles slightly, like a slightly off-center spinning top. This precession is due to the gravitational influences of the moon and sun, which cause the Earth to bulge slightly at the equator. Just to complicate matters, there is also an **apsidal** precession, which creates a wobble of the orbital ellipse. The combined effect of the axial and apsidal precessions result in a precession cycle of approximately 23,000 years. These three types of orbital changes are the key drivers of long-term temperature and climate variations. They are also responsible for the beginning and ending of the Ice Ages. Serbian Milutin Milankovic has combined the effects of these cycles to create a mathematical model for calculating the amount of solar radiation reaching the Earth at different latitudes along with corresponding surface temperatures.

[36] Who was Milutin Milankovic? He was a Serbian mathematician, astronomer, climatologist, geophysicist, civil engineer and author. Born in 1879 in the small town of Dalj, he and his twin sister were the oldest of 7 children. His three brothers all died of tuberculosis and his father died when Milan was eight years old. Milankovic made two grand contributions to global science. The first was the "Canon of the Earth's Isolation", which characterizes the climates of the planets in the solar system. The second was an explanation of Earth's long-term climate changes caused by variations in Earth's position relative to the Sun. These changes are commonly referred to as Milankovic cycles and give an explanation of ice age cycles.

Milutin Milankovic
Ⓢ Public Domain
File: Milutin Milankovic 2.jpg
Created: 1920s date QS:P,+1920-00-00T00:00:00Z/8

[37] **How do ice cores reveal past temperatures and CO_2 concentrations?** Ice cores provide a unique view of past climate history because bubbles within ice cores capture gas concentrations of years past, which give scientists information about ancient history; the same way that tree rings shed light on Earth's recent past. In order to obtain this information, scientists have to travel to ice sheets in Greenland or Antarctica and by using a special drill, are able to drill into the ice a depth of up to 3.7 km (roughly 3 miles). In the Polar Regions, where mechanical drills are used, rotating barrels with a cutters at the head will continue to drill until the barrel is filled. The barrel length determines the length of the ice core and can range between 1 and 6 meters. The diameter can vary from 5 to 14 cm. Once these samples have been procured, scientists slice them up in sections, and then study the composition of the section's gas bubbles by crushing the ice section in a vacuum. Because layers of snow that fall in different seasons have different textures, winter snow will have a different chemistry than summer snow. These ice cores (proxies) can tell scientists about temperature, precipitation, atmospheric composition, volcanic activity and even wind patterns.

[38] Glaciers are formed when snow becomes ice after being compacted over seasons and years by the snow above it. Particulates and chemicals collected by falling snow become part of the ice's history. Layers in the ice cores corresponds to different years and seasons with the youngest ice at the top of cores and the oldest at the bottom. These ice cores contain the historical record of hundreds of thousand years in a very high resolution. Because of this high-time resolution and the ability to archive greenhouse and non-greenhouse gas concentrations from the past, ice cores have become the gold standard for paleoclimate research.

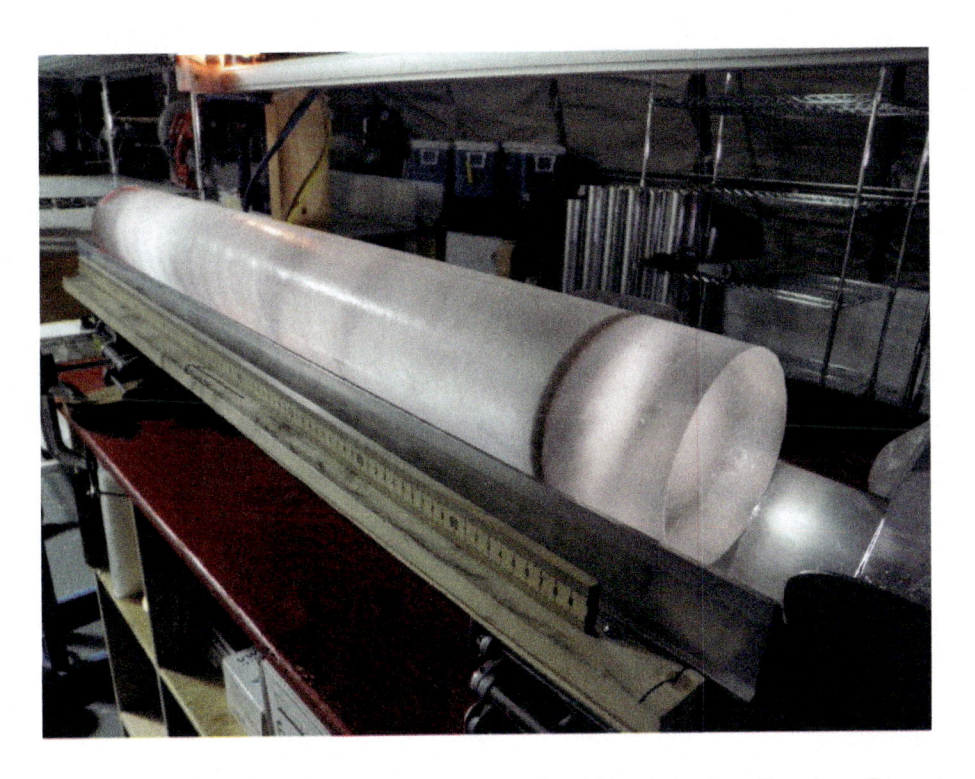

The dark band in this ice core from the West Antarctica Ice Sheet Divide (WAIS Divide) is a layer of volcanic ash that settled on the ice sheet approximately 21,000 years ago. Credit: Heidi Roop NSF

[39] **Global CO_2 concentrations:** The world's most meaningful and reliable data collection installation of global CO_2 concentrations is on the slopes of Mauna Loa volcano on the big island of Hawaii. Both NOAA and the Scripps Institution of Oceanography make independent measurements from this station located at an elevation of 3430 m (11,240 ft). Note: These measurements began in 1958 and data has been uninterrupted until a massive volcano eruption on November 27, 2022 halted data collection. Lava has covered the road leading up to the monitoring station and the reopening of the station is unknown. However, recent data shows a rapid increase in CO_2 concentrations over the last 60+ years.

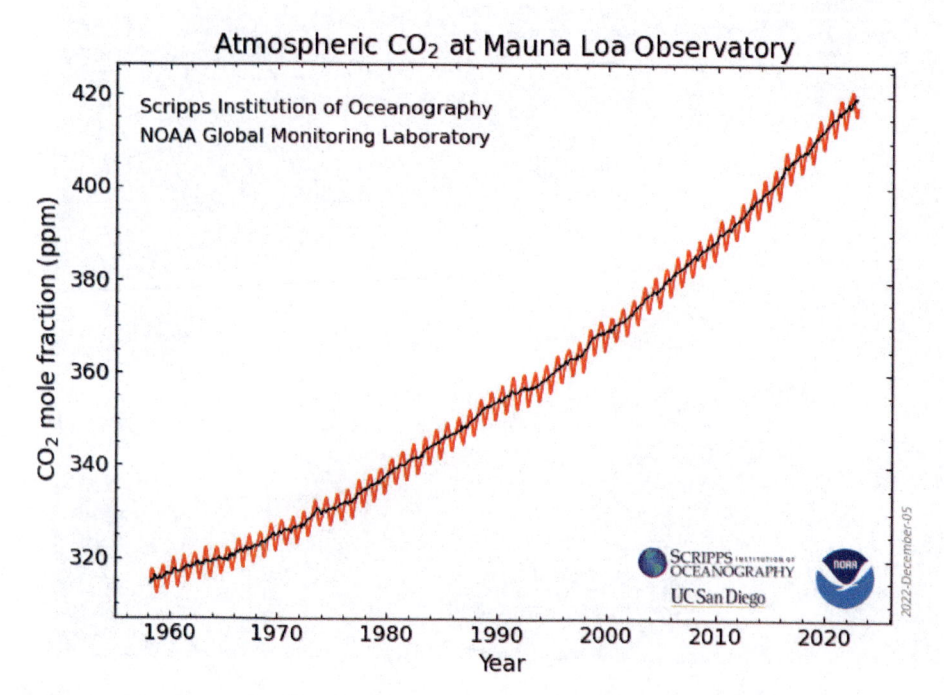

Atmospheric CO₂ at Mauna Loa Observatory

Scripps Institution of Oceanography
NOAA Global Monitoring Laboratory

[40] Other CO_2 monitoring stations include NASA's satellites OCO-2 and OCO-3. OCO-2 circles the Earth from pole to pole and OCO-3 is attached to the International Space Station (ISS) which orbits between 52° degrees latitude north and 52° degrees latitude south. Additional sentinel satellites are the European Space Agency's METOP-A and TROPOMI platforms, China's TANSAT and Japan Space Agency's GOSAT and GOSAT-2. The satellite data and data from Mauna Loa are all in agreement; **CO_2 concentrations are increasing at an alarming rate and correspond to the temperature increases in both atmospheric and surface monitoring.**

[41] **How has the ocean responded?** The ocean is the Earth's largest heat sink and plays a major role in absorbing and storing heat. The ocean, which covers 70% of the Earth's surface can

absorb large amounts of heat without large increases in temperature. On the other hand, the atmosphere can show significant increases in temperature while storing a small amount of heat. Why is this? The air or atmosphere has a very low heat capacity (specific heat; 1.0035 J). The heat capacity of water is considerably higher (specific heat; 4.18 J) Because of the ocean's ability to store and release heat, it plays a major role in stabilizing the Earth's climate system. Waves, tides and currents constantly mix the ocean's waters, moving heat from warmer to cooler latitudes and to deep parts of the ocean. The heat, although moved in this great liquid laboratory does not disappear, but stays in the ocean. This ocean heat energy will eventually be released into the Earth's system by melting glaciers, ice shelves or evaporating water. Remember that according to the Second Law of Thermodynamics, heat will move in one direction only; from hot to cold.

[42] **How is ocean heat measured?** Historically, measuring the ocean's heat required ships to drop sensors into the ocean or to collect water samples. Considering the vastness of the world's oceans, this was a poor way to measure ocean heat. With the advent of satellites, global coverage of the Earth's oceans has been achieved by measuring the height of the ocean's surface. Since water expands when heated, a measurement of heat content could be deduced. In addition, scientists use **in situ** temperature sensing instruments that can measure temperature at different depths. Among these are a fleet of roughly 3,000 Argo floats, which are sensors that descend the ocean's depths and measure temperature and salinity as they ascend. Periodically, according to programmed instructions, they rise to the surface and send this information and their location to satellites and then descend again. There are many different models of these floats, but on average they are about 5 feet long, 8 inches in diameter and weigh about 72 pounds. Even

seals have been fitted with sensors in areas that are difficult for instruments to reach. Scientists then process this information every three months to calculate an estimate of the ocean's global heat content. This estimate is then converted to Joules which allows comparison to other parts of the Earth's climate system.

NASA Argo float (October 6, 2012) by Maria Jose Vinas

The above float is at the ocean's surface and is awaiting instructions to descend to more than 3000 feet (914 meters).

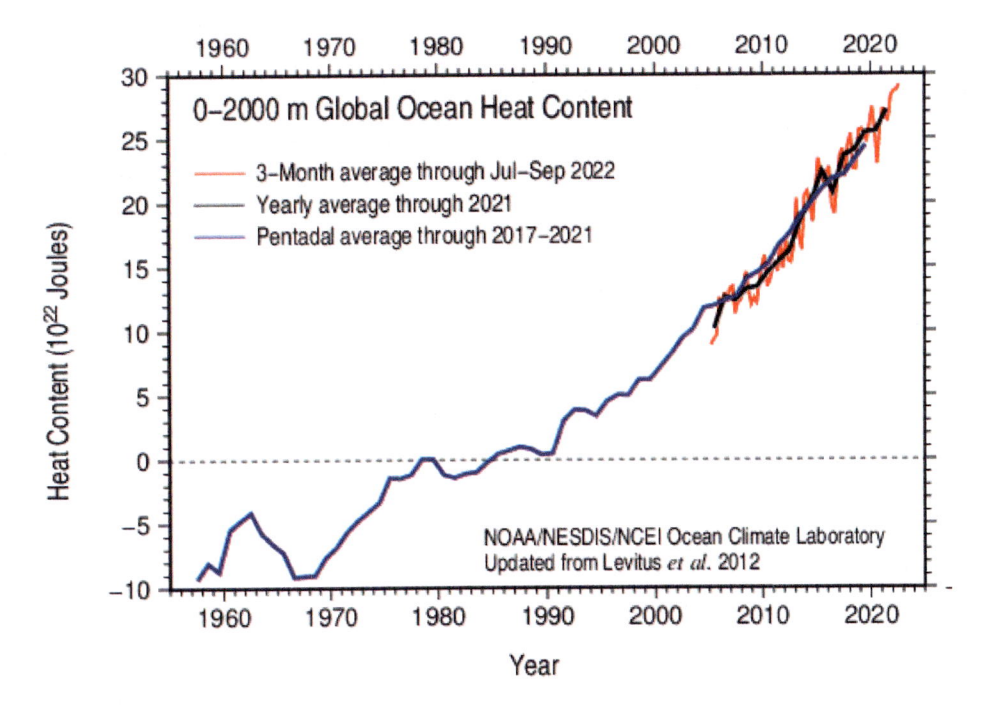

[Figure: 0–2000 m Global Ocean Heat Content, NOAA/NESDIS/NCEI Ocean Climate Laboratory, Updated from Levitus et al. 2012. Shows 3-Month average through Jul–Sep 2022, Yearly average through 2021, and Pentadal average through 2017–2021, with Heat Content (10^{22} Joules) on y-axis from -10 to 30, and Year on x-axis from 1960 to 2020.]

[43] **Change over time**: Collected data indicates that 90% of Earth's warming over the last 50 years has occurred in the ocean. Recent studies have shown that 63% of the ocean's heat content is stored in the top 700 meters. About 30% is stored from 700 meters down to the ocean's floor. This global energy imbalance means that while the atmosphere has been spared from much of the global warming, heat already stored in the ocean will eventually be released, which means additional Earth warming in the future.

Ocean Acidification: Why it matters? Billions of people depend on the ocean for food, recreation and transport. Without a healthy ocean, coastal economies would be crippled and starvation would be rampant. In the last 200 years, the pH of ocean surface waters has fallen by 0.1 pH units. This doesn't seem like much, but because pH is measured on a logarithmic scale, this change represents a 30% pH decrease and a 30% increase in acidity. The pH scale runs from 0 to 14 with 7 being neutral. Anything higher than 7 is alkaline and anything lower is acidic. When carbon dioxide is absorbed into the ocean, the ocean water (H_2O) combines with CO_2 to produce carbonic acid (H_2CO_3). This weak acid breaks down (dissociates) into hydrogen ions (H^+) and bicarbonate ions (HCO_3). The pH scale is the inverse of the hydrogen ion concentration, so more CO_2 absorption means more hydrogen ions, more acidity and a lower pH. In 2022 the average pH level of the ocean's surface was 8.1. NASA scientists estimate that if the ocean continues to absorb CO_2 at the current rate, that by 2100 the pH level of the ocean would be 7.8; a number that low would have last been observed in the middle Miocene glacier period, about 14-17 million years ago.

[44] Sometimes called the **"osteoporosis of the sea"**, ocean acidification is causing a chemical imbalance of the Earth's oceans from pole to pole. This chemical imbalance creates conditions that can eat away at minerals used by oysters, lobsters, clams, shrimp, coral reefs and other marine life to build their shells and skeletons. In addition, people can become ill eating contaminated shell fish, sickened fish and marine mammals. Harmful algae produce more toxins and bloom faster in acidic waters, posing a real concern for human health. Increased acidification of our oceans can upset the balance of microscopic life in every drop of ocean water. Portions of the United States that will be hit the hardest by this acidic increase include the Pacific Northwest, Long Island Sound, Narragansett Bay, Chesapeake Bay, Gulf of Mexico and areas off the coasts of Maine and Massachusetts. Also at risk are the fisheries in Alaska, which account for 60% of the US commercial fish harvest that support 100,000 jobs. Because the cold waters in the Antarctic are able to hold vast amounts of CO_2, shelled creatures tend to dissolve in these corrosive conditions, affecting the food sources of fish, birds and marine mammals. In the future, decreased harvests

of marine life will disproportionately affect the poorest and least developed countries, especially those with fewer agricultural alternatives. This could eventually lead to mass migrations to more urban areas, causing social disruption and conflict.

[45] The **speed** at which ocean acidification is occurring is the dominant issue that will affect humans in the near future. Scientists initially thought that the absorption of CO_2 by the world's oceans was a good thing, since it mitigated the temperature increases occurring in the air and on land. Today, this rapid absorption of carbon dioxide is referred to as the "evil twin" of climate change and in 2003, the term "ocean acidification" was first coined. Geologists have been able to dig into the Earth's distant past by studying cores of soil and rock samples taken deep into the Earth's crust. Some of these samples go back 65 million years. From these samples, geologists are able to determine when carbon dioxide and temperatures were similar to conditions existing today. No past events replicate what scientists are seeing today. Marine life has evolved over millions of years in an ocean with a relatively stable pH. But this latest rapid increase in ocean acidity is not giving marine life much time to adapt. The chemical impacts are predictable, but the biological impacts are not. Some species will adjust and thrive; others might go extinct. Humans and economies will be forced to adapt.

Chapter 9
Glacier National Park in Pictures

When Glacier National Park was established in 1910, it contained over **100** named glaciers. In 2022, after considerable melting of the glaciers due to global warming, about **25** were large enough to be considered glaciers. I began teaching math and physics at St Petersburg College in the year 2000, and immediately became absorbed in the causes and possible remedies of global warming. I began giving yearly seminars in 2001 on the Clearwater, FL campus and was known around campus as a global warming crusader. On **March 6, 2011**, my wife Joyce and I decided to visit Montana and see the glaciers for ourselves. I would then use our experience as the foundation for my yearly seminar on global warming. We had never been to Montana and were excited to visit the northern portion of the Rocky Mountains that had a much different climate than what we were used to in sunny Clearwater. We arrived on the outskirts of Whitefish, Montana and promptly headed to the Good Medicine Lodge, which would be our living quarters for the next five days. [46] Note: all photographs of the events in Montana were taken with a small Chinese pocket camera (3 ½" x 2"), 7.0 megapixel G1, by the author.

Entering Whitefish, Montana (population, 6,352 in 2011)

Upon arriving we were treated to oatmeal raisin Big Mountain, Montana cookies.

On day number two, we are on a ski lift headed toward the top of Big Mountain.

Big Mountain Elevation 6,817 feet

We are nearing the top of Big Mountain with a view of Whitefish Lake from our ski lift.

Whitefish Lake

Joyce at the top of Big Mountain with Glacier National Park in the background

Joyce enjoying the ride and the view

The camera person who was directing John was trying for an uplifting photo.

However, John is blocking the view of the Park.

Preparing for the trip down the mountain

The skiing was invigorating!

The following morning we were disappointed to learn that the only road into the Park (Going-to-the-Sun Road) **was closed**, due to weather conditions. We **were unaware** that this road seldom opens before June. However, some good fortune and great weather were on our side. Driving near the Park's entrance, I noticed a helicopter parked in the driveway of a roadside home. There were no signs of tours, but I decided to knock on the door adjoining the driveway and inquire about the possibility of flying into the Park. The helicopter's owner was a small, hearty man in his 70's, who primarily used his copter to recue lost hikers. After some **considerable negotiations**, he agreed to fly us among these extraordinary mountain peaks.

Our four-seater transportation into Glacier National Park

Our very experienced pilot (Jerry) noted that the weather conditions for this time of year (March) were **phenomenal** (usually cloudy), with snow or blizzard conditions common, but on this day the climate gods were with us and visibility was roughly **50** miles. In the photo below, we are following the highway that passes in front of Jerry's house and are approaching the west entrance to the Park.

Hovering above the road and headed to the Park

Factoid: In 2010, there were approximately 300 grizzlies in the Park. At the time of Lewis and Clark there were 50,000. Along with its magnificent views, plant diversity and wildlife, this national treasure truly deserves the name "**Crown of the Continent**"

The west entrance

The temperature when we left Jerry's driveway was 32°F (0°C). The reader should know that **none** of the following photos have been **color-enhanced or photo shopped** in any way. The pictures are exactly as they appeared after an upload from my tiny camera to my computer.

Getting closer

We are currently flying 50 yards from the mountain peaks. Jerry seems to know the Park like the back of his hand. To get this close to these magnificent peaks requires an experienced and daring pilot plus great weather. Because of glacier melt due to global warming, photos such as these will **likely never happen** in the future. A fearless pilot, great weather, 2011 and a slightly nervous photographer combined to capture these once-in-a-lifetime views.

And closer

We are flying at roughly 10,000 feet and according to our pilot, the temperature is 23°F (-5°C).

Mt. Jackson (10,300 feet)

I am sitting in the shot-gun seat next to Jerry with my feet on two metal foot rests. The bottom portion of the helicopter is open, so the air temperature inside the copter and outside are the same. I'm concerned that with my cold hands, I might drop my camera. Fortunately, that did not happen. Otherwise these pictures would have been lost in the valley below.

Mt. St. Nicholas – 9,600 feet (pyramid in shape and very popular with climbers)

Just before this shot was taken, we spotted a **bald eagle** flying along beside us at roughly 9,000 feet.

Jackson Glacier – on the north side of Mt. Jackson

Factoid: Lake McDonald is the largest fresh-water lake in the Park and fills a basin carved out by ancient ice age glaciers. The lake is surrounded by mountains on the north, south and east. It is commonly thought that that lake is named after a fur trader named Duncan McDonald, who carved his name on a nearby tree in 1878.

Lake McDonald – 14 miles long and 4 miles wide, 450 feet deep.
Note the snow-capped mountain reflection.

After an exhilarating helicopter ride and having captured breathtaking views of the Park, we are finally back on **flat** land with a view of what else? Flathead Lake.

Flathead Lake with Glacier National Park peaks in background

Bigfork, Montana: It seems like a good place for some refreshment after our fascinating journey through the Park.

Grizzly Jacks – One of many saloons and casinos all over Montana; a license is all that is needed.

Grizzly Jacks was sold in 2014 to a Texas couple who have remodeled the log building into their private residence and added space for retail and commercial offices for their American Airboat business. They purchased the property for $499,000.

Inside Grizzly Jacks – Note Joyce in the background to the left of the window.

After our adventure in the air, Joyce and I decided to do some exploration on land. Just for fun, an after a 2 hour drive, we arrived in Fernie, Canada.

Fernie, Canada – Main Street; population in 2011, 4,594; in the background, note the Glacier National Park mountain peak.

On the road back to Whitefish, Mt.

Entering Montana

In October 18, 2011, I gave my annual seminar on global warming during All-College Day on the Clearwater campus. I created a PowerPoint highlighting the pictures I had taken of the mountain peaks and glaciers in Glacier National Park. In front of a standing-room only crowd, I warned of the consequences of human greenhouse gas emissions and how it had affected one of our spectacular national treasures. **My original intent was to compare pictures I had taken with photos of the Park in 1900.** However, comparable photos were not available. However, my seminar was well received and encouraged me to pursue the installation of solar panels and electric car charging stations on campus.

The installation of solar panels became a reality on November 13, 2013, when flexible thin-film solar panels were installed on the roof of the Clearwater campus National Science Building. This was two years after my "glacier melt" seminar. Electric car charging stations and an additional 100 kW solar panel installation would soon follow.

Chapter 10
Thoughts of Scientists and Intellectuals

Many books have been written about global warming and climate change. **Some** are serious books written by climate scientists who attempt to explain complex climate systems to non-scientists. A **few** books are written by **experts** in the field, who are able to draw some meaningful conclusions about the Earth's changing climate. These books may often present the science erroneously as **certain or settled**. These conclusions based on certain science can then be used by governments, politicians and the media to communicate an invalid point of view to the public. Most of these books are not read or purchased by the general public, because they are too complex for the average reader. However, there is one book that is written by an expert in the field of climate science that has been widely read and whose ideas and conclusions about **global warming** are rigorously presented. Those who have an interest in our planet's health should read it. The book is titled *Unsettled* and the author is Steven E. Koonin.

Steven E. Koonin
Under-Secretary for Science of the US Department of Energy
Ⓢ Public Domain
File: Steven Koonin official portrait.jpg
Created: 1 January 2009

Unsettled is a *New York Times* best seller and the Wall Street Journal calls it Amazon's "Best science book of 2021, so far". The book was released on April 27, 2021 and the publisher BenBella

Books, Inc., estimated that it might sell 15,000 books, but by December 2021, it had sold 100,000 books. *Unsettled* has had great reviews from the vast majority of readers including an impressive list of scientists. **One of the few zealous critics** of the book is Mark Boslough, a former physics student of Koonin. Mark claims that Koonin's title hints at a logical fallacy called the "strawman" (see glossary) argument and this early statement on the cover's flap confirms the argument. "When it comes to climate change, the media, politicians and other prominent voices have declared that the science is settled". Mark's expertise however, is **not** in climate science, but in planetary collisions and global catastrophes. Mark does have a PhD in physics and is a frequent critic of other writings outside his expertise. The book *Unsettled*, however, is impressive, but the author's **credentials may be more impressive.**

[47] Steven E. Koonin was born in Brooklyn, NY and graduated from high school at 16. He received his BS in physics from the California Institute of Technology (Caltech) and his PhD from the Massachusetts Institute of Technology (MIT) in theoretical physics. When he joined the faculty at Caltech, he became one of their youngest professors. He then served as the provost from 1995 to 2004. He later took on the role of chief scientist at British Petroleum (BP) in charge of the company's long-range strategy in technology, in particular alternative and renewable energy sources. He was appointed Under-Secretary of Science during the Obama administration, serving from 2009-2011. He is currently the director of the Center for Urban Science and Progress at NY University. He has been a consultant for the National Science Foundation, the Department of Defense and the Department of Energy. His research interests include the areas of nuclear physics, computational physics, nuclear astrophysics and global environmental science. Koonin has written one other book titled

Computation Physics which was published in 2018 by CRC Press, LLC.

[48] The following are examples of what a few leading scientists and intellectuals have written about Koonin's book *Unsettled*.

"[Unsettled] should be on the reading list of scientists and engineers whose responsibility, as citizens, extends beyond the laboratory to communicating to a larger public often overwhelmed and confused by the media." – Jean-Lou Chameau, President Emeritus of Caltech.

"We have too many global warming books – but this one is needed. Steven Koonin has the credentials, expertise, and experience to ask the right questions and to give realistic answers." – Vaclav Smil, Distinguished Professor Emeritus at the University of Manitoba.

"Essential reading and a timely breath of fresh air for climate policy. The science of climate is neither settled nor sufficient to dictate policy. Rather than an existential crisis, we face a wicked problem that requires a pragmatic balancing of costs and benefits." – William W. Hogan, professor of global energy policy at Harvard Kennedy School.

"Tough talk about climate politics from a statesman scientist – and a sobering vision of the future." – Robert B. Laughlin, professor of physics at Stanford University.

"Unsettled will definitely and rightly unsettle your climate thoughts, and all for the better. If we are to make trillion dollar investments, we deserve to be as well informed as possible." – Bjorn Lomborg,

President of Copenhagen Consensus and fellow at the Hoover Institution at Stanford University.

The reader should keep in mind that global warming, not climate change is the subject of *Earth Plight* and the first part of Koonin's book *Unsettled,* deals with the Earth's warming. I will detail some of the data and observations given in part I of *Unsettled* to reason that the Earth **is warming** and to what degree (no pun intended).

Koonin reveals to the reader early on that there is **no certainty** in climate science and that all science is unsettled. This is probably obvious to many readers, since a changing world requires a revision of ideas that result in modifications to the science. On the subject of global warming and without previous evidence, Koonin makes this sweeping statement on page 1 of his introduction. "Yes, it's true that the globe is warming and that humans are exerting a warming influence upon it." Koonin goes on to say, after attending an American Physical Society (APS) workshop, that "Humans exert a growing, but physically **small**, warming influence on the climate. The deficiencies of climate data challenge our ability to untangle the response to human influences from poorly understood natural changes".

Small compared to what? The use of the subjective word small tends to minimize the effect that a warming Earth has on our planet. The alarming part of global warming is the **rate of the increase.** If you are to believe the various proxies available to today's paleoclimatologists, the rate of this warming is unlike anything observed in history going back millions of years. The proxies of ice cores and rock samples do show greater warming, but at a rate at least 10,000 times **slower** than today. With less time to adjust to this unprecedented warming, humans, aquatic and land animals face an uncertain future.

In an effort to sway public opinion, many prominent climate activists have made outrageous statements that gives insight into their motives. Three disgraceful samples follow:

"It doesn't matter what is true, it only matters what people believe is true." – *Paul Watson*, cofounder of Greenpeace

"We've got to ride this global warming issue. Even if the theory of global warming is wrong, we will be doing the right thing in terms of economic and environmental policy." – *Timothy Wirth*, President of the UN Foundation

"Some colleagues who share some of my doubts argue that the only way to get our society to change is to frighten people with the possibility of a catastrophe, and that therefore it is all right and even necessary for scientists to exaggerate. They tell me that my belief in open and honest assessment is naïve." – *Daniel Botkin*, former chair of Environmental Studies at the University of California at Santa Barbara

[49] The 6th assessment report (AR6) by the Intergovernmental Panel on Climate Change (IPCC) was released by **working group I (WGI)** on August 9, 2021. WGI examined the **physical science** supporting past, present and future climate change. WGI consists of 234 leading scientists from around the world who have donated their time to contribute to AR6. The IPCC was formed in 1988 and I will primarily focus on observations and statements in the report that involve **global warming.**

[50] The first part of the WGI report makes this statement which aligns with information presented in previous chapters. "It is **unequivocal** that human influence has warmed the **atmosphere, ocean and land**. Widespread and rapid changes in the atmosphere, ocean,

cryosphere and biosphere have occurred." AR6 also affirms with **high confidence** that the last four decades have been the warmest since 1850; that greenhouse gas (GHG) increases since 1750 are due to human activities; that human influence are the likely drivers of the global retreat of glaciers since 1990 and the decrease in spring snow cover in the Northern Hemisphere. The WGI adds that since the release of the 2014 5th assessment report (AR5), improvements have been made in both data collection and information from paleoclimate archives that reinforce this warming. The reader should note the word **unequivocal** in the WGI report, which means a very high confidence level. The WGI presents this graph to show that human influence has warmed the climate at an **unprecedented rate** for the last 200 years.

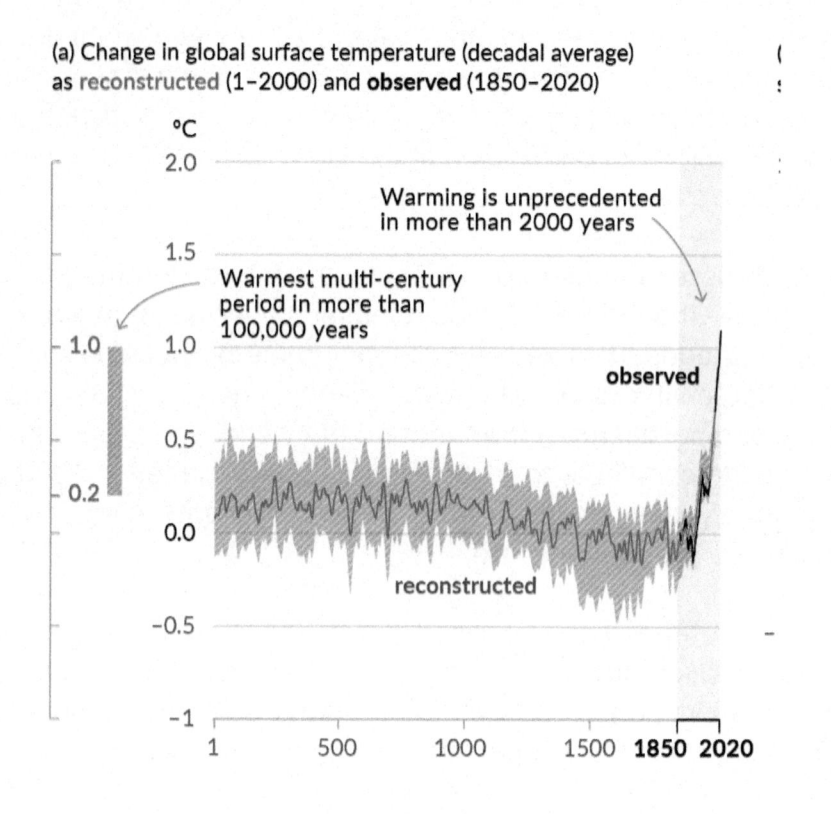

(a) Change in global surface temperature (decadal average) as reconstructed (1–2000) and observed (1850–2020)

Warming is unprecedented in more than 2000 years

Warmest multi-century period in more than 100,000 years

observed

reconstructed

The global surface (air, land and ocean) temperature increases illustrated in the graph from years 1-1850 are reconstructed from **paleoclimate archives** and the warming from years 1850-2020 are from **direct observations**.

[51] In the next section WGI examines observations that in some respects **are more alarming than the first section**. "Global surface temperature will continue to increase until at least mid-century under all emissions scenarios considered." Other assertions in the AR6 report made by the WGI group and related to global warming were: Changes in the climate system will become larger in response to increasing global warming and include reductions in Artic sea ice, snow cover and permafrost; with projected CO_2 emissions, ocean and land carbon sinks will become less effective in slowing the increase of CO_2 in the atmosphere. Then there is this sobering statement. "Many changes due to past and future greenhouse gas emissions are **irreversible for centuries to millennia**, especially changes in ocean, ice sheets and global sea levels."

I wholeheartedly agree with Koonin on the importance of the world's ocean as an indicator of global warming. Koonin asserts that the ocean holds more than **90% of climate's heat** and has a "long-term memory". Changes in the Earth's atmosphere can vary widely from month to month or year to year, but the ocean normally responds to changes over decades or centuries. Even though data collection and analysis of the world's ocean is challenging, it is constantly improving. The warming of the Earth's ocean is real and the rate of warming is unmatched in our planet's history.

It is well known that water vapor is the most important greenhouse gas, but its concentration varies with the location and the weather. The next most influential greenhouse gas is CO_2 and its concentration is relatively constant all over the globe. Since 1960, the carbon dioxide concentration has increased from 315 parts per million (ppm) to 420 ppm in 2022, and continues to increase at a rate of over 2 ppm every year. There is universal agreement among climate scientists that this increase in CO_2 is a result of human activities, in particular the burning of fossil fuels. Another potent GHG is methane (CH_4) but it only stays in the atmosphere for roughly 12 years before it combines with ozone (O_3) to form carbon dioxide and water. The resultant CO_2 will continue to heat the atmosphere for hundreds or even thousands of years. The NOAA and Scripps graph on page 62 is sometimes referred to as the **Keeling Curve**, named after scientist **Charles David Keeling** who began the recording of atmospheric carbon dioxide concentrations at Mauna Loa Observatory in 1958. This data collection remains the world's longest continuous record of CO_2 concentrations.

President Bush presents the Medal of Science to Charles Keeling
Ⓢ Public Domain
File: Charles David Keeling 2001.jpg
Created: 1 January 2001

Steven Koonin makes an **interesting point** about climate changes occurring in the United States (US), saying that temperatures are **getting milder**. After asserting that the US has the world's most extensive and highest quality weather data, Koonin claims that **daily record high temperatures** are no more prevalent today than they were a century ago, **but record lows are less common**. He says it this way. "There have been some changes in temperature extremes across the continuous United States. The annual number of high temperature records set shows no significant trend over the past century nor over the past forty years, but the annual number of **record cold nights has declined** since 1895, somewhat more rapidly in the past thirty years."

[52] Concerning milder temperatures, climate scientist Camilo Mora of the University of Hawaii (UH) at Manoa states it somewhat differently. In a 2013 article published in the journal *Nature*, Mora defines the term "**climate departure**", Camilo says that the time will come in the 21st century when all locations around the world will reach a point where the climate is much different than anything that has existed throughout human history. Mora states: "Here we present a new index of the year when the projected mean climate of a given location moves to a state continuously **outside the bounds** of historic variability under alternative greenhouse gas emission scenarios." The layman translation is: **Record lows in a given location will no longer be set, only record highs.**

In a phone conversation with Mora on January 10, 2023, I asked Camilo about recent developments in his projections of **climate departure**. He responded this way. "The models indicate that many locations around the world will experience climate departure earlier than what was projected in 2013." Because the human influences since 2013 has been greater than anticipated, some locations in the tropics will experience departure much earlier.

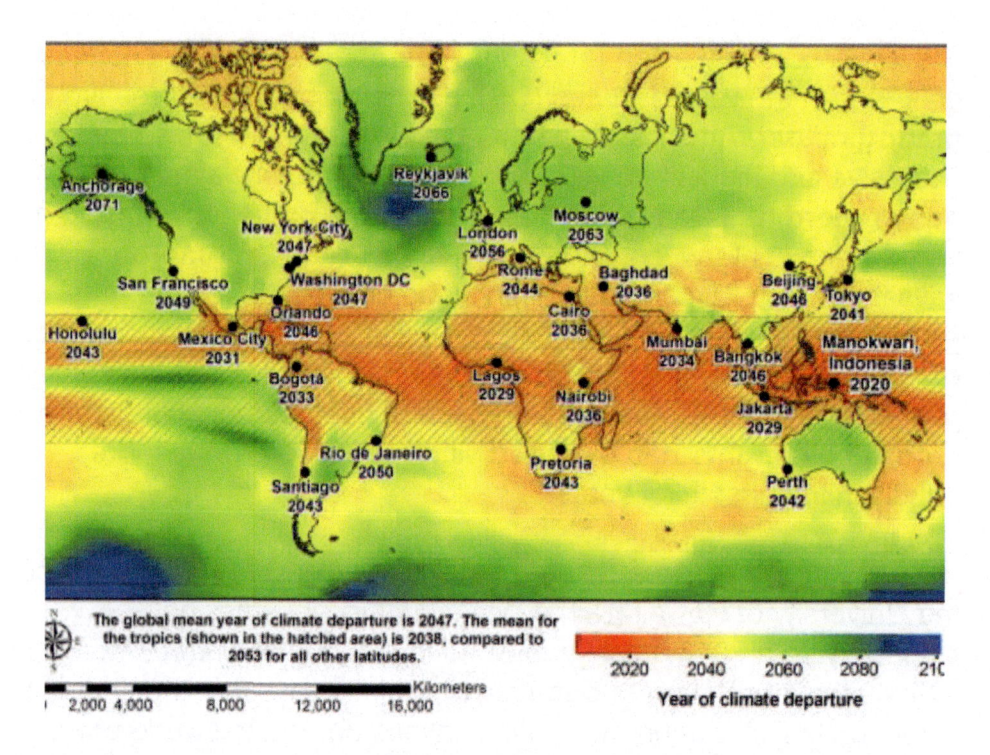

The global mean year of climate departure is 2047. The mean for the tropics (shown in the hatched area) is 2038, compared to 2053 for all other latitudes.

Note that world map shows that the global-mean year of climate departure is **2047**, but the mean for the tropics is 2038. On the edge of the tropical zone is Orlando, FL at **2046**.

Camilo Mora

Will the Earth reach a time when the planet's climate no longer resembles what has existed throughout human history? According to climate scientist Camilo Mora, the answer is **yes**. He strongly believes that in the near future, heat records will be routinely broken and what was once considered extreme will become the norm.

Mora claims that climate departure will occur sooner in the tropical regions (2038) than at the poles. When asked why, he responded. "The reason for that is that the tropics have a very **small** variability. So it's very easy for climate change to move the climate in the tropics beyond anything the tropics have seen. In the tropics, the species are adapted to a very stable climate. So as soon as you move the climate beyond the variability, all the species in the topics are going to suffer quite dramatically. And we already have evidence of that. Coral reefs are a good example. If you increase the temperature by just one or two degrees, there is massive bleaching and coral mortality." Camilo feels that all the species that live at the poles have already adapted to the variability there. Mora feels frustrated that repeated warnings about rising temperatures are routinely ignored.

Camilo has always had a huge interest in communicating to the general public the harmful effect of increasing global temperatures due to human activities. According to Mora, "I have taken many courses for my undergraduate degree and my Ph.D., but I never took a class in how to communicate science to the general public." Camilo believes that barriers have been created in recent years, making it even harder to communicate climate science to today's youth. He feels that today's young minds want quick answers and social media platforms such as Twitter, TikTok and Meta have made the dissemination of science more difficult.

[53] Mora believes that helping people understand the relationship between current climate disasters and greenhouse gas emissions should be a priority for every climate scientist. "That's the million dollar question. How do we speak to people in a way that we get them to appreciate the significance of these problem?"

Einstein's official portrait after receiving Nobel Prize in 1921
©Public Domain
File: Albert Einstein (Nobel).png
Created: 1 circa 1921 date QS:P,+1921-00-00T00:00:00Z/9,P1480,Q5727902

Albert Einstein may **not** have spent a lot of time thinking about global warming, but he did spend a lot of time thinking. The formulation of special relativity, general relativity and quantum mechanics occupied a considerable portion of his time. He also found time to postulate the famous equation $E = mc^2$. In 1921, he was awarded the Nobel Prize in physics for his discovery of the photoelectric effect. Einstein died in 1955 when global warming was not yet a hotly debated topic, but some of his thoughts on human stupidity are relevant to today's global warming problem.

[54] "We can't solve today's problems with the mentality that created them."

"The difference between genius and stupidity is that genius has its limits."

"Two things are infinite: the universe and human stupidity; and I'm not sure about the universe."

[55] **Enrico Fermi** was one of a very few scientists that excelled in both theoretical and experimental physics. He won the 1938 Nobel Prize in physics for his work on induced radioactivity and has been considered the architect of both the nuclear age and the atomic bomb.

[56] Enrico also advanced the **Fermi Paradox** which refers to the conundrum between the high probability that extraterrestrial intelligence exists and the fact that no evidence of their existence has been found. The British science-fiction author Sir Arthur C. Clarke said it this way. "Two possibilities exist: Either we are alone in the universe or we are not. Both are equally terrifying."

Some scientists have advanced the idea of a **Great Filter** that might prevent civilizations from advancing far enough to make contact. Catastrophic events like climate change, asteroid impact or nuclear Armageddon could wipe out intelligent life before they would have a chance to extend their reach among the stars.

Enrico Fermi in 1943
©Public Domain
File: Enrico Fermi 1943-49.jpg
Created: between 1943 and 1949 date

Another possibility is that aliens have observed us and found us too primitive to contact. Consider this analogy. You are walking on a sidewalk and spot an anthill. Do you stop and try to communicate with the ants? Probably not. You might study them for a while, but unless you are a myrmecologist, your study will probably be short-lived.

Elon Musk is likely to go down in history as the greatest innovator and visionary of the 21st century. He is the founder of Tesla and SpaceX and at one time was the world's richest man. He is a firm believer that humanity's future lies beyond our planet Earth. Three of his more famous quotes are below.

[57] "There's a fundamental difference, if you look into the future, between a humanity that is a space-faring civilization, that's out

there exploring the stars...compared with one where we are forever confined to earth until some eventual extinction happens."

"I would like to die on Mars. Just not on impact."

"The extension of life beyond earth is the most important thing we can do as a species."

NASA administrator Charles Bolden congratulates **Musk** in front of the SpaceX Dragon following its successful 2012 mission.
Ⓢ Public Domain
File: Charles Bolden congratulates SpaceX CEO and chief designer in front of the historic Dragon capsule.jpg
Created: 13 June 2012

Stephen Hawking: English theoretical physicist and cosmologist.

[58] "I don't think the human race will survive the next thousand years, unless we spread into space."

"We are in danger of destroying ourselves by our greed and stupidity. We cannot remain looking inwards at ourselves on a small and increasingly polluted and overcrowded planet."

"I would like **nuclear fusion** to become a practical power source. It would provide an inexhaustible supply of energy, without pollution or global warming."

NASA StarChild image of Stephen Hawking
Ⓢ Public Domain
File: StephenHawking.StarChild.jpg
Created: 3 January 1999

Chapter 11
The Harsh Reality

*I*f the previous discussions about our warming planet have not convinced you (the reader) that global warming is real; maybe the description of life in Jacobabad, Pakistan will. [59] Jacobabad's record high temperatures continue to increase and the impoverished population of roughly 200,000 at a latitude of 28.3°N, continues to suffer. It has the reputation as being one of the hottest places on Earth, having reached a record temperature of 126°F (52.2°C) in the shade. The week before *Time* reporter Aryn Baker arrived in Jacobabad on June 29, 2019, the temperature reached 124°F (51.1°C) and the city regularly surpasses 122°F (50°C) in the summer months. To avoid the heat, tractors till the soil at night and farmers take breaks from noon to 3 pm. One young woman who toiled daily in the rice field explained it this way, "Even when it's 52°C to 53°C, we work, or we don't get paid." Others in the city say that if life stopped every time the temperature surpassed 104°F (40°C), nothing would ever get done. Concerning the recent (July, 2022) deadly heat waves in Europe, Camilo Mora was asked if record temperatures in Paris (108°F) might become the new normal in Europe. He laughed. "The new normal is likely to be far worse. It's likely to look something like Jacobabad." Climate scientists estimate that the planet's temperature (emissions as usual scenario) will likely increase 3°C by the end of the 21st century. That would likely result in record high temperatures of 131°F in Jacobabad and 114°F in Paris. Currently, outdoor restaurants in Jacobabad are open only at night. Even though there are hotter places in sparsely inhabited, desert locations, like Death Valley, CA; record temperature of 134°F (57°C), Jacobabad is starting to consistently pass the temperature threshold that humans can withstand. This threshold known as the wet bulb temperature is a combination of temperature and humidity. The theoretical limit of human survival in the shade, with unlimited water is a wet bulb temperature of 35°C (95°F) equivalent to a heat index of 70°C (160°F). Water evaporates only when the air can absorb more water. As the air temperature increases, air reaches a point where it can no longer absorb water. This wet bulb temperature happens when the relative humidity is 100%.

[60] It's not just Jacobabad that is having to adjust to record heat. The Australian Tennis Open held in Melbourne each year has its own rules concerning heat. These rules were first established in 1998 and have undergone several changes since. The current rule gives the weather a rating of 1 to 5, which combines air temperature, radiant heat of the sun, humidity and wind speed. In 2023, play on day 2, was suspended on all outdoor courts because heat conditions were considered unsafe for players and spectators. In 2014, the tournament had four consecutive days with highs

between 41.5 and 43.9°C (106.7 and 111°F), but the humidity remained low enough that play was suspended on only one day. The tournament's decisions to suspend play for only one day was widely criticized by both players and spectators. One player, Canadian Frank Dancevic, who collapsed after his first round loss, called the conditions "inhumane". Another player who collapsed and was forced to retire, feared he might die in the extreme conditions. A total of nine players retired on the tournament's second day. The French player Jo-Wilfried Tsonga and Denmark's Caroline Wozniacki noted that their shoes and water bottles were beginning to melt. On the third day of the tournament 970 fans had to be treated for heat exhaustion and the record heat resulted in 9 withdraws in the first round. The latitude of Melbourne is 38.9 degrees south, making it the same latitude north as Baltimore, MD.

What then is the harsh reality? The Earth's warming is accelerating. Our over-populated planet keeps producing more people. The population is aging exponentially. One-third of the planet is hungry and food insecure. Pollution is rampant and increasing. Nuclear weapons have the potential to wipe out our civilization. Wars among governments continue. The risks of super volcanos are real. The economic chasm between rich and poor continues to increase. Rising sea levels threaten many coastal cities. Deforestation continues. Natural resources are facing depletion. Earthquakes, tornados, hurricanes and forest fires continue to claim lives and wreak destruction at an increasing rate. The global community's knowledge and interest in global warming can be aptly compared to a 'half-opened book in a dimly lit room'.

[61] The warming and cooling of the Earth depends on the amount of sunlight (solar radiation) reaching the surface of the earth and the amount of greenhouse gases in the atmosphere. Other than water vapor which stays relatively constant, the most important driver of

the earth's warming is the amount of CO_2 in the atmosphere. And because it can last for centuries or even thousands of years, it must be addressed in conversations about current global warming. According to ice core samples, the Earth has experienced regular ice ages related to the Earth's orbit around the sun and changes in the Earth's axis of rotation (Milankovitch cycles). We are currently in a warm cycle (interglacial) between ice ages. Ice ages did not happen for millions of years because there was too much carbon dioxide in the atmosphere. When CO_2 is above 300 parts per million (ppm), the subtle changes due to the Milankovitch cycles are overwhelmed and ice ages do not develop. About three million years ago, CO_2 levels dropped below 300 ppm and the ice age cycles began. The current carbon dioxide level is above 430 ppm and rapidly rising, so if humanity continues to overload the atmosphere with more carbon emissions, the next ice age will be a long time coming. Humans will likely live in a warmed climate for generations to come.

[62] According to NASA, the Milankovitch cycles cannot explain the rapid warming that is presently under way on planet Earth. "Scientists are confident that Earth's recent warming is primarily due to human activities – specifically the direct input of carbon dioxide into Earth's atmosphere from burning fossil fuels." Since the beginning of the Industrial Age, the carbon dioxide in our atmosphere have increased 50%; from 280ppm to 420 ppm. During the last million years CO_2 levels have never exceeded 300 ppm until today. Climate models demonstrate that the Earth's climate due to the Milankovitch cycles are bypassed when CO_2 levels exceed 350 ppm. The amount of solar radiation falling on the Earth has increased very little in the past 100 years and is therefore not a significant driver of the Earth's current climate warming. **"Finally, Earth is currently in an interglacial period (a period of milder**

climate between Ice Ages). If there were no human influences on climate, scientists say Earth's current orbital positions within the Milankovitch cycles predict our planet should be cooling, not warming, continuing a long-term cooling trend that began 6,000 years ago."

And that's not cool.

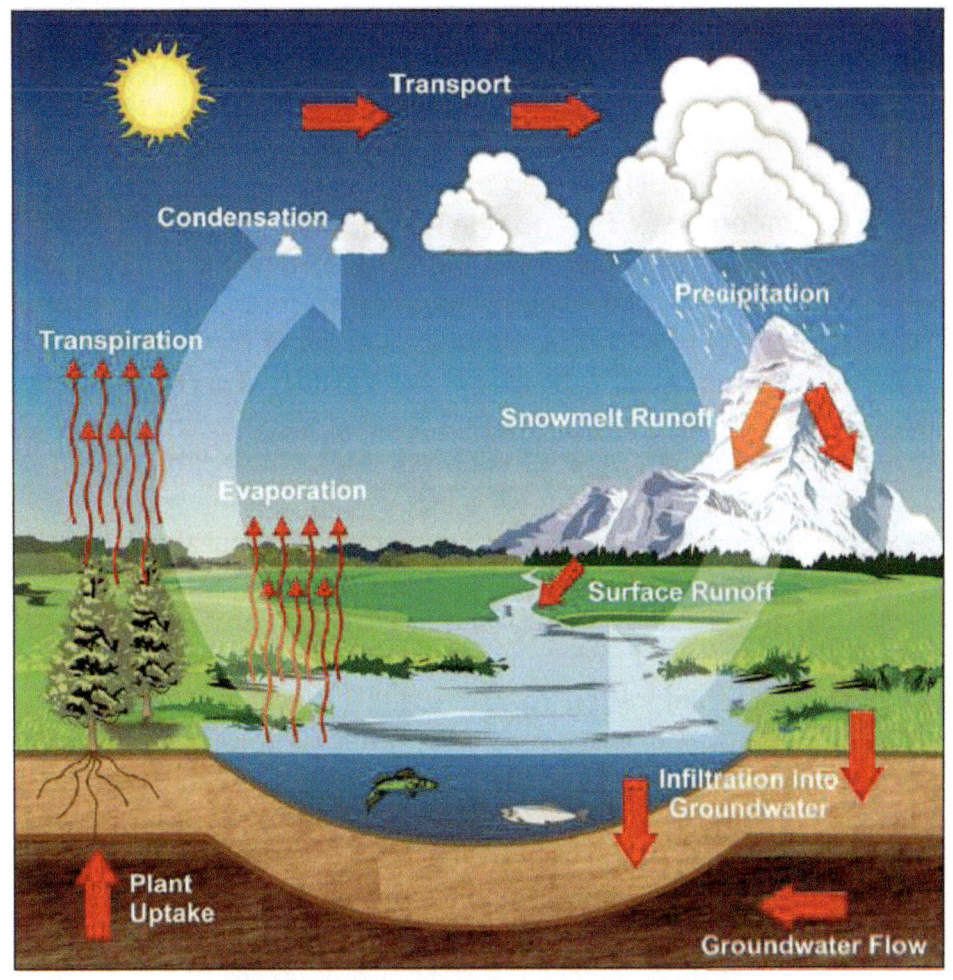

Earth's Water Cycle. Credit: NASA

The reader should remember from previous discussions that the total amount of water and water vapor on planet Earth is **nearly** constant, since the Earth's gravitation field is strong enough to keep both from escaping into space.

Some pundits in the media have incorrectly declared, "We know the **planet** is getter hotter and **drier**." Even though some locations may experience droughts; others may experience floods. **Most water and water vapor cannot escape the Earth's gravitation field.**

Record Temperature expected in 2023-2025: [63] On May 3, 2023, the United Nations (UN) warned that the world should be prepared for rising temperatures. El Nino (the **warming** of the sea-surface waters of the equatorial Pacific) is expected to develop in 2023 and usher in new heat records worldwide. Wilfran Moufouma Okia, who is the UN head of the World Meteorological Organization (WHO), made this statement about the effects of El Nino. "This will change the weather and climate patterns worldwide." Even though the past three years have seen record temperatures in many parts of the globe, the cooling effect of La Nina (the **cooling** of the sea-surface waters of the equatorial Pacific) has somewhat moderated the extreme temperatures that have been recorded in 2021-2023. Once the full effect of El Nino is established in the Pacific, **dangerous heat waves** will likely threated the lives of both animals and humans. WMO chief Petteri Taalas had this to say about the La Nina and El Nino. "La Nina acted as a temporary brake on global temperature increases." He added, "The world should prepare for the development of El Nino."

[64] **The Melting Artic Sea Ice:** Scientists predict that the Artic Sea Ice will disappear in the 2030's, a decade earlier than previously anticipated. Climate scientist Dirk Notz, a professor at the University of Hamburg's Institute of Oceanography disclosed to the

Agence France-Presse (AFP) this alarming prediction. "It is too late to still protect the Artic summer sea ice as a landscape and a habitat. This will be the first major component of our climate system that we lose because of our emission of greenhouse gases." Without the Artic sea ice, a majority of the Sun's radiation will be absorbed by the Arctic Ocean, instead of being reflected back into space. Both the North and South Pole regions have warmed by 3°C (three times the global average) compared to late 19th century levels.

HOT! HOT! HOT! How hot will it get? What follows is the opinion of the author and is based on data from NASA, NOAA and WMO. Because of the predicted strength of El Nino and the continuing carbon emissions being produced by an expanding global population, heat records will be routinely broken during the next three years (2024-2026). Florida will have **triple-digit** temperatures as early as May, and July and August with be particularly brutal. Even the summer thunderstorms that regularly occur in Florida, will not slow the record-breaking temperatures. Cold temperature records will likely be a **thing of the past**. Climate departure in Florida's interior will occur sooner than the dire predictions of UH climatologist Camilo Mora. The Gulf of Mexico's summer water temperature will set new heat records and further damage Florida's fragile coral system. Because of an increase in the vertical wind shear caused by El Nino, the good news for Florida will be **fewer hurricanes**. Instead, California will bear the brunt of tropical hurricanes due to the warming of the sea-surface waters of the Pacific. **Drought and floods** will devastate parts of mainland United States. Global temperatures will soar. During the three-year period after 2026, the effect of La Nina will slightly moderate the heat-related consequences of El Nino. After 2028, what happens next will not be pretty.

Chapter 12
Are There Solutions?

Yes, there are solutions. But in order to find the best solutions, we will follow the advice of Albert Einstein. That advice was to spend the majority of your time defining the problem and then the solution should be easy. [65] His exact quote was, "If I were given one hour to save the planet, I would spend 59 minutes defining the problem and one minute resolving it." Solutions are often contained in a well-defined problem; or at least made obvious. In the first 11 chapters, I have tried to define the problem associated with the unprecedented heating of our planet and I will summarize the problem in three parts.

Problem #1: Human activities have released a **glut of carbon dioxide** in the atmosphere that threaten our civilization. Carbon neutrality is needed.

Problem #2: Our current means of producing **electrical energy** is both polluting and not sustainable. The **wants** of the majority of the world's population continues to demand increasing amounts of electrical energy

Problem #3: Human population growth continues to threaten Earth's ability to **feed and shelter**.

Solution to problem #1: Carbon Neutrality is the desired outcome, but how can it be achieved? [66] University of Hawaii professor Camilo Mora and his daughter have a simple solution; **PLANT TREES; DON'T CUT DOWN TREES!** What is carbon neutrality? Carbon neutrality happens when our CO_2 emissions equal emissions removed. Trees absorb carbon dioxide and through a process called photosynthesis grow and flourish. Trees use CO_2 as fuel and give off oxygen as a byproduct. The CO_2 is then stored in the tree and soil. By using the energy from the sun (solar radiation), carbon dioxide combines with water to produce glucose and oxygen. The chemical formula is:

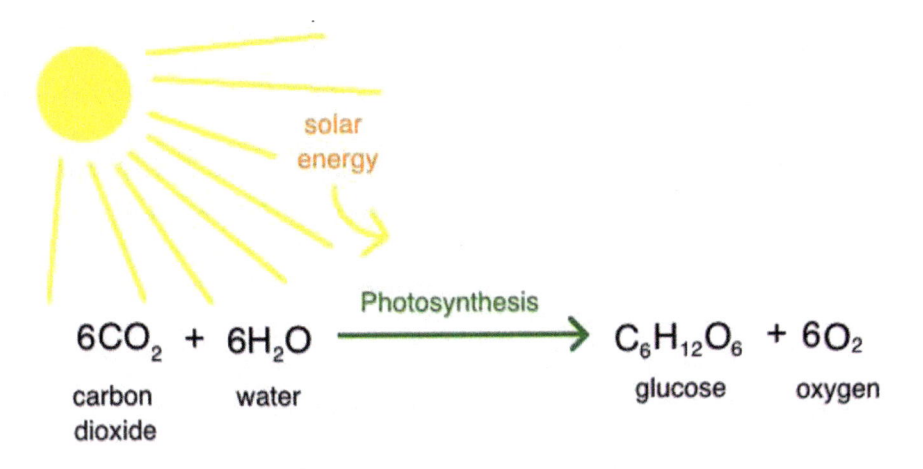

$$6CO_2 + 6H_2O \xrightarrow{\text{Photosynthesis}} C_6H_{12}O_6 + 6O_2$$

(solar energy)

carbon dioxide + water → glucose + oxygen

The idea of a '**Carbon Neutrality Challenge**' was the brainchild of his daughter, Asryelle, who at age seven said to her dad, "Let's plant trees," and the challenge was born. Mora and a devoted group of followers are committed to planting one million trees a year on the island of Oahu. In only two hours, Mora and his 2,000 volunteers were able to plant 10,000 trees. He feels this proves he can get to a one million trees per year, which would make Hawaii the first state to become carbon neutral. Part of his plan is to build at least 50 portable greenhouses that can produce 20,000 seedlings per year. Increasing a seedlings survival rate is an important key to achieving his goals. "In our latest plantings …two months after a tree is planted, we rarely get a tree dying." Mora has also reduced the cost of tree seedlings, from $4 per tree to $.15 per tree. [67] How many trees need to be planted to offset our carbon emission? MIT professor Charles Harvey has made some approximations that puts this solution in perspective.

- The average American's carbon footprint is around 16 tons/year.
- One mature tree absorbs about 50 pounds of carbon/year.
- It would take 640 trees/person to offset America's contribution. This adds up to 200 billion trees.
- Presently, there is an estimated 3 trillion trees on the Earth.

The additional piece of the solution is the **'don't cut down trees'** part. Governments around the world need to follow Mora's lead and expand tree planting and limit **deforestation**. The world's largest rainforest by far is the **Amazon Rainforest** and deforestation is rampant. In the **first half of 2022**, NASA satellite monitoring has recorded a record of 1,500 sq. miles deforested in the Amazon (an area 5 times the size of NYC). [68] One reason for the continued devastation is the policies of Brazilian president Jair Bolsonaro, who took office in 2019 and has allowed deforestation to surge with no end in sight. In the last 50 years, 17% of the Amazon has been destroyed and 64% lies within the borders of Brazil. Cattle ranching is the single biggest cause of deforestation in the Amazon and accounts for 80%. The forest is cleared for farmers to raise cattle, primarily for exporting beef. In addition to meat, there is also an international demand for leather, dairy and cosmetics. The Brazilian Amazon is home to 200 million head of cattle and is the largest exporter of cattle products in the world, supplying one quarter of the global market. In addition, scientist estimate that those 200 million cows will give off 44 **trillion** pounds of methane per year.

Ariel view of Amazon deforestation – Credit: Iuoman

[69] Another major contributor to deforestation is the construction of **roads** into the Amazon, in particular the **Trans-Amazonian**

Highway, which runs through the center of the Amazon Rainforest. Upon the highway's opening in 1972, deforestation, along with **devastating wildfires**, spiked. The highway allows small-scale subsistence agriculture to flourish and these landowners have been blamed for much of the rainforest's destruction. One landowner claimed that they had no choice and said this. "Even if you take a deserted area you have to clear, burn and make a house where you can live with your children. You're not going to make a house in the hollow of a tree, as if you were a bird, right?" Building materials need to include less wood and lumber companies should pay more in taxes. Much of Midwestern United States were once covered in dense forests; trees could grow there again. There is plenty of available land around the world to double our current tree population; 3 trillion trees could easily become 6 trillion trees if we had the will. **"The forest grows where no human goes."**

Solution to problem #2: Many different approaches (wind, solar, oil, coal, natural gas, nuclear fission) are being tried to solve our electrical energy **wants** with limited success. The world's electricity-producing power plants account for over 50% of the carbon dioxide pumped into our atmosphere. **Could Hydropower dams** be **the solution** to our electrical wants? On the surface they appear to be non-polluting, renewable and sustainable, but a close examination of operational dams in our treasured rainforests suggest the opposite. Dams contribute to **deforestation** by replacing large tracts of forest with extensive reservoirs of water. In 2020, there were over 150 dams in the Amazon with hundreds more planned. These hydroelectric plants produce inexpensive electricity that is crucial for poor countries to develop economically. However, these plants come with crushing costs to the Amazon and other rainforests around the world. **This has to stop.** When damming major tributaries to rivers like the Amazon and the Nile, wildlife habitats are destroyed, indigenous people are displaced and populations downstream are left with less water that over time becomes increasingly toxic. These huge projects are touted as being both **renewable** and **reliable**, but the reality is that they are neither. When reservoirs fill, upstream forests flood, which eliminate their function as a carbon sink. Decaying plants and trees in tropical rainforests become carbon emitters and emit an estimated one billion tons of greenhouse gases annually.

File: 09 09 2021 Visita a Unsina Hidrelectrica Belo Monte (51443381900).jpg
Created: 9 September 2021

The largest hydroelectric plant in the Amazon is the **Belo Monte Dam** pictured above and as the reader can see on the next page, the amount of electricity generated depends on the time of year. The Dam is located in Brazil on one of the major tributaries (Xingu River) of the Amazon River. During the rainy season (January – June), the reservoir is full and electricity is plentiful. During the dry season (August – November), the electricity is reduced to less than 1,000 Megawatts (MW) per month.

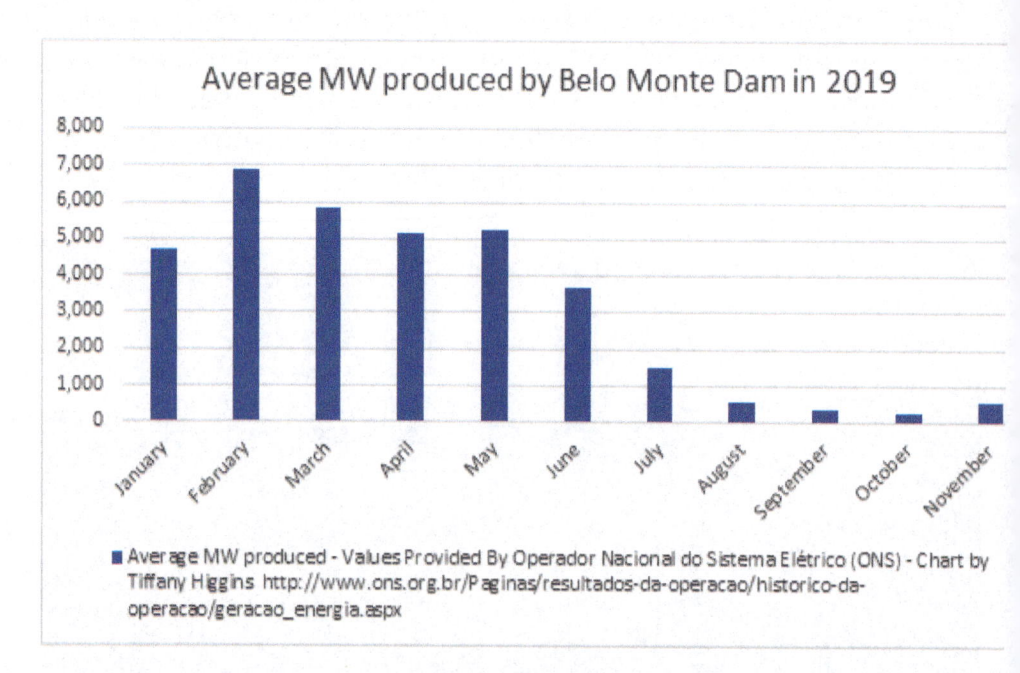

Average MW produced by Belo Monte Dam in 2019

■ Average MW produced - Values Provided By Operador Nacional do Sistema Elétrico (ONS) - Chart by Tiffany Higgins http://www.ons.org.br/Paginas/resultados-da-operacao/historico-da-operacao/geracao_energia.aspx

This Belo Monte Dam is the world's 5th largest hydroelectric project with a reservoir of 260 square miles. Large dams often have a short lifetime, because as the submerged forest rots, the water becomes acidic and will eventually corrode the dam's turbines. A major complication concerns ownership. Who owns the rights to the Amazon forest and the Amazon River? The Amazon spreads into nine countries: Brazil, Columbia, Peru, Venezuela, Ecuador, Bolivia, Guyana, Suriname and French Guiana. These are poor countries having governments eager to improve the lives of their citizens. Therefore, every country wants their 'fair' share of the rainforest's treasure and will go to extreme lengths to dam major tributaries of the Amazon River that are within their country's borders. The Amazon River is the second largest river in the world with a length of over 4,000 miles, flows east to west, has 1,100 tributaries and empties 20% of the world's freshwater into the Atlantic Ocean. Other major dams in the Amazon are:

Balbina Dam – 1,200 square mile reservoir.

Tucurui Dam – 1,110 square mile reservoir.

Samuel Dam – 168 square mile reservoir.

Because of deforestation and a sharp increase in **wildfires, the Amazon Rainforest** is now a **net carbon emitter**, instead of a **major carbon sink**. The Amazon now emits about a billion tonnes of carbon dioxide per year equal to the annual emissions released in Japan, the world's 4th largest emitter. Forest fires alone create three times more carbon than the forest can absorb. **Can the Nile River present a possible solution?**

Nile Delta from Space with Red Sea to the right and Nile to the left.
Ⓢ Public Domain
File: Nile River and delta from space.jpg
Created: 5 February 2003

[70] The Nile River, considered to be the world's longest river (4,130 miles) runs south to north and empties into the Mediterranean Sea. The Nile travels through the **Congo Basin Rainforest** (1/3 the size of the Amazon), and runs through 11 countries listed below.

The Democratic Republic of the Congo,
Tanzania
Burundi
Rwanda
Uganda
Kenya
Ethiopia
Eritrea
South Sudan
Republic of Sudan
Egypt.

The construction of the controversial **Great Ethiopian Renaissance Dam (GERD)** on the **Blue Nile** was started in 2011 and once completed will have a generating capacity of **6.5 GW**, which would make it the third largest in the world. Ethiopia aspires to be Africa's largest electricity exporter and claims the dam is central to its economic development. The Blue Nile, with its headwaters at **Lake Tana in Ethiopia**, supplies 85% of the water to the Nile River. The **White Nile** with its headwaters at **Lake Victoria** supplies most of the rest. The desert country of Egypt claims that the GERD is an existential threat to its water supplies. [71] In 2022, hydroelectric power accounts for **16%** of the **total electricity** generated worldwide. **Nuclear** accounts for **10%. Solar and wind** account for **8%. Fossil fuels** account for **63%**. The largest hydroelectric power plants are in China which produce roughly **6%** of the total hydroelectric power. The next largest producers are Brazil, United States and Canada.

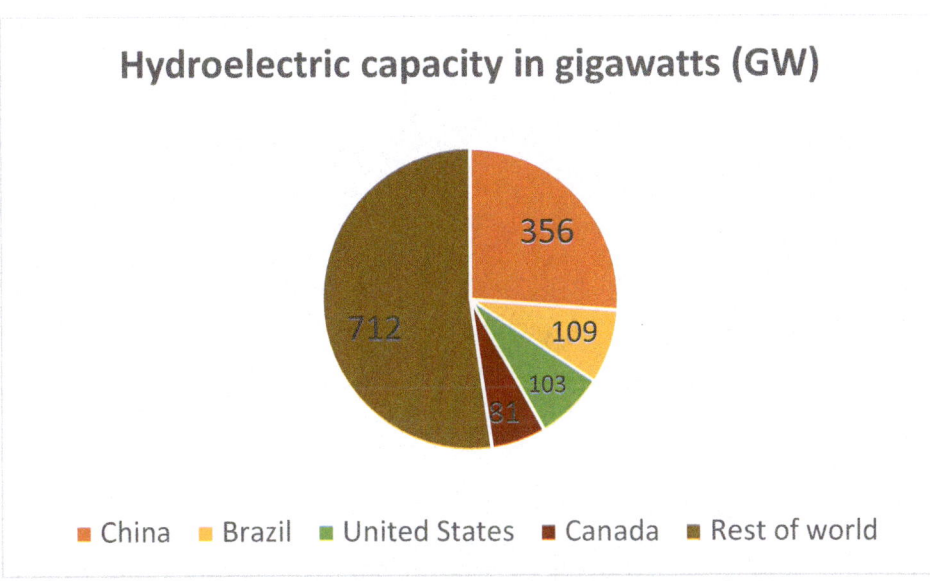

Hydroelectric capacity in gigawatts (GW)

- China: 356
- Brazil: 109
- United States: 103
- Canada: 81
- Rest of world: 712

Pie chart created by Williams, J. R. Statistics from *BizVibe*

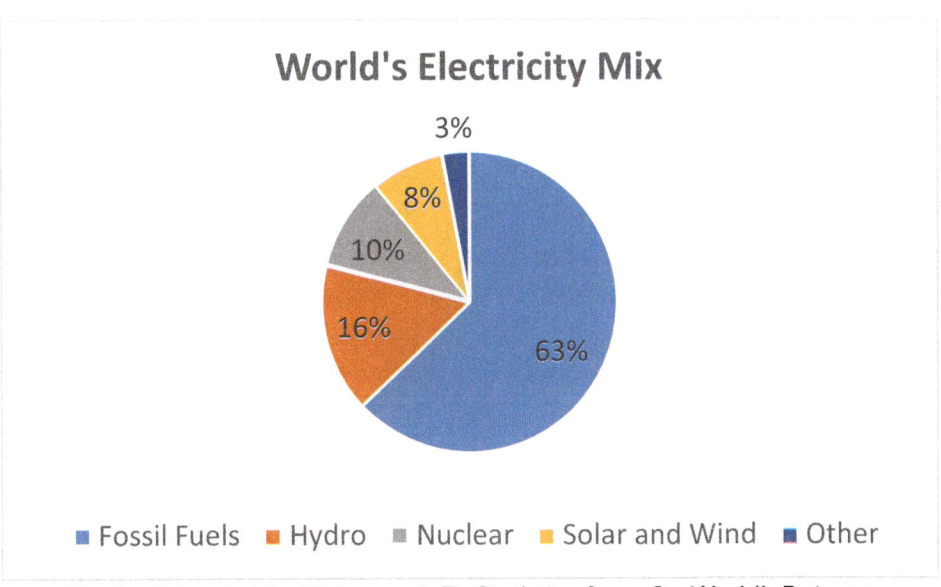

World's Electricity Mix

- Fossil Fuels: 63%
- Hydro: 16%
- Nuclear: 10%
- Solar and Wind: 8%
- Other: 3%

Pie chart created by Williams, J. R. Statistics from *OurWorldInData.org*

Blue Nile Falls fed by *Lake Tana* near city of Bahir Dar, Ethiopia
File: ET Bahir Dar asv2018-02 img17 Tis Issat.jpg
Created: Savin, Alexander. 5 February 2018

[72, 73] China has the **two largest** dams in the world. The **Three Gorges Dam (22 GW** installed capacity) is the largest and spans the Yangtze River. The second largest is the **Baihetan Dam (16 GW)**, which spans the Jinshaw River. China's President Xi Jinping has claimed that electricity produced by hydroelectric power will allow China to achieve net-zero carbon emissions by 2060.

The **United States** has greatly reduced their number of coal-fired power plants in operation. However, **China**, in spite of their increases in hydroelectric power, has done the opposite. With a steady stream of new coal-fired power plants coming online weekly, plus a large number in the planning stages, [74] China continues to be the largest carbon dioxide emitter, accounting for **31%** of the world's total.

Victoria Falls at the headwaters of the *White Nile*
Ⓢ Public Domain
File: Victoria Falls.jpg
Created: 14 February 2005

Efforts of governments around the world to increase hydroelectric production, while well-intended, appear to be counterproductive and will not make a dam (pun intended) bit of difference.

What is needed is an **unlimited, inexpensive energy source with no pollution**. In the not so distant future, **nuclear fusion** may offer a much needed solution. The words cheap, affordable, clean, renewable, carbon neutral, sustainable and unlimited are often used to describe electricity producers, but there are no current means of achieving these goals.

However, Controlled Nuclear **Fusion** has the potential to satisfy human's **unlimited want** of electrical energy. [74] A breakthrough in nuclear fusion technology occurred on December 5, 2022, when the Lawrence Livermore National Laboratory announced that it had achieved a net gain in a controlled-fusion reaction. A net gain occurs when more energy is produced that what was used to trigger the reaction. Nuclear power plants currently use a **fission reaction** to release the energy that is stored in nucleus of an atom. This energy that binds protons and neutrons together in an atom's nucleus is released when a heavy atom such as uranium is split into two smaller radioactive fragments. A **fusion reaction** occurs when two light nuclei are fused together to produce a heavier nucleus. A fusion reaction is much harder to induce because the lighter nuclei must be heated to roughly 100 million degrees Celsius in order to overcome the electrical repulsion that hinders their fusion. This fusing together of the smallest atoms in the universe releases a tremendous amount of energy with temperatures approaching that of our Sun. Both **fission** reactors and **fusion** reactors are the energy sources that heat water to produce steam that turn turbines to produce AC electricity. However, **fusion** reactors can produce clean, green, safe, reliable, emission-free electrical energy using an unlimited supply of fuel.

[75] There are several tech billionaires who are betting that fusion reactors can deliver this unlimited supply of fuel that the world so desperately wants. Thirty-eight year old Sam Altman heads an impressive list of billionaires who are betting that the process powering the Sun and stars can be harnessed to satisfy mankind's **want** of limitless energy. Other billionaires that have invested heavily into fusion technology include Bill Gates, Jeff Bezos, Peter Thiel, and March Benioff. Altman, who is the CEO of **OpenAI,** has been one of Silicon Valley's most prolific investors for more than a decade. OpenAI is an American Artificial Intelligence (AI) research

laboratory consisting of the non-profit OpenAI Inc. and its for-profit subsidiary corporation OpenAI Limited Partnership. Mr. Altman has made the biggest financial bet of his career on the futuristic startup **Helion Energy Inc**.

[76] The race for clean-energy solutions to replace fossil fuels is rapidly gaining momentum and fusion power is seen as the leading candidate. Other associated technologies and applications that are being pursued are powerful magnets and improved lasers. Marc Benioff, the CEO of **Salesforce Inc**. has invested in the Massachusetts Institute of Technology (MIT) spinout called **Commonwealth Fusion Systems** (CFS). CFS plans to build compact power plants and counts Bill Gates as a large investor. Mr. Benioff gushes that fusion is a "tremendous dream. It's the Holy Grail. It's the mythical unicorn." Marc was persuaded to become a major investor by **Sun Microsystems** co-founder Vinod Khosia. Mr. Khosia, who was an early fusion-power investor, believes that large superconducting electromagnets can be successfully designed and built in the near future. These large electromagnets would be crucial to making fusion power a reality. Mr. Khosia sees his investment in fusion power this way. "Financially, you either lose one times your money or you can make a thousand times your money. That's the math of fusion." Mr. Benioff adds that, "Fusion has no limits if you can get it to work."

[77] **Microsoft enters deal with nuclear fusion company Helion Energy.** Microsoft has made a gamble on nuclear fusion technology by agreeing to purchase electricity from Helion Energy Inc. within five years. Helion has agreed to sell at least 50 megawatts (MW) of electricity produced by nuclear fusion by 2028. If Helion is unable to produce 50 MG, financial penalties will be imposed. Microsoft President Brad Smith explained his reasoning by saying, "We wouldn't enter into his agreement if we were not

optimistic that engineering advances are gaining momentum." Sam Altman, who is a major investor in Helion Energy, gave this explanation of Helion's goal. "The goal is not to make the world's coolest technology demo. The goal is to power the world and to do it extremely cheaply." Mr. Altman went on to say that having a first customer for fusion power is critical for keeping Helion grounded in the realities of the business.

[78] Microsoft President Brad Smith believes that in the next decade, fusion power, artificial intelligence (AI) and quantum computing will benefit from unprecedented innovation and might "intersect" with each other. Both AI and quantum computing will require extensive amounts of electricity that nuclear fusion could provide. Mr. Smith added. "As a purchaser, when we lean in at the right moment in the right way we can help make new markets." The optimism of Helion Energy CEO David Kirtley was enthusiastic when he proclaimed the readiness of fusion energy. "We think the physics of this is ready for us to signal the commercialization of fusion."

Solution to problem #3: There is a growing consensus among scholars and scientists that technology alone will not be able to satisfy the **wants and needs** of a constantly expanding global population. The human population depends on the Earth's ecosystem for survival and this relationship between man and nature has been thrown out of balance. Currently **consumption** and **pollution** are overwhelming our planet. This is what we know.

Climate change is constant and will continue.
Migration of humans and weather will continue.
Floods, Drought and **Heat Waves** will continue.
A polluting population chasing the **almighty dollar** will continue.
World population on July, 2023 was just over **8 billion**.

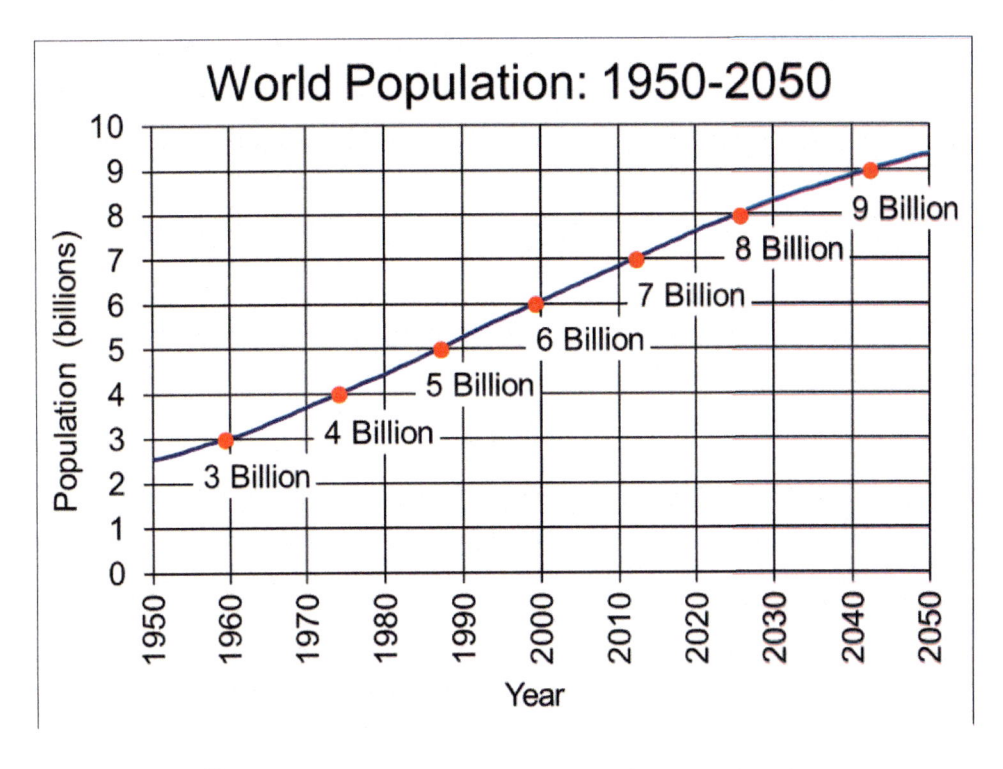

[79] World Population Graph by *Researchgate*

[80] Around 1800, the human population reached one billion. By 1925, it was 2 billion. By 2023 it was over 8 billion and is projected to reach 10 billion by 2056.

[81] Billionaire Elon Musk has tweeted on several occasions that "population collapse due to low birth rates is a much bigger risk to civilization than global warming." However, Joseph Chamie, who is a former director of the United Nations Population Division, said this about Musk's views of population collapse, "He's better off making cars and engineering than at predicting the trajectory of the population." It is likely that Musk was referring to the financial collapse of society and not how an increase in birth rates might

impact the environment. Elon's view seems to be that the problem of too many mouths to feed is secondary to the dilemma of too few people to work. Elon has stated multiple times that he plans to colonize Mars and make humans a space-faring species. [82] "It's important to get a self-sustaining base on Mars because it's far enough away from Earth that [in the event of a war] it's more likely to survive than a Moon base." Musk added, "If there's a third world war, we want to make sure there's enough of a seed of human civilization somewhere else to bring it back and shorten the length of the dark ages." Musk has also cited the risk of asteroid strikes, world-wide pandemics and "AI gone wrong".

As early as 1996, media mogul Ted Turner had the right idea about how to control an expanding global population. His solution was to reduce the global population **voluntarily** to about 2 billion people. Of course, it's not sheer numbers that determine the impact on our planet, but how much we consume and how much we waste. Ted did not supply a lot of detail on how voluntary population control (VPC) could be achieved, but he was on the right track when it comes to dealing with a population that continues to over-consume and pollute. There are ways to achieve stabilization and ultimately reduction of the human population in a civilized way. These methods are well-known and inexpensive. They are education for women everywhere. Free contraception made available for everyone. The social, political and financial incentives for large families need to be eliminated. This should apply to both the wealthy and the poor. But merely reducing fertility rates in order to achieve a population contraction will not create a sustainable future for mankind. Consumption and pollution must also be reduced. We must shrink pollution, while reducing consumption. The views of Ted Turner and Elon Musk appear to be at odds; Ted calls for VPC and Elon maintains that more people are needed to keep civilization from collapse. Industrialized countries tend to consume and pollute. Developing countries consume less and pollute less. The intersection of quantum computing, nuclear fusion and AI has the capacity to benefit civilization in remarkable ways. Clean, nuclear waste-free, reliable, inexpensive and virtually unlimited electricity supplied by nuclear-fusion reactors will allow billions to consume energy in the form of electricity without carbon emissions. Pollution, however will remain a problem. Society must shrink the amount of pollution. Cars, batteries, glass and plastics must be recycled. Anything that is not biodegradable needs to be either recycled or not produced. This is where artificial intelligence can be helpful. AI will have the ability to diagnose and prescribe the best way to curtail our pollution problem.

Summary: The world's climate scientists report that the Earth is warming at an unprecedented rate and is caused by human activities. Reforestation instead of deforestation can help. Dam building to produce hydroelectric power, while initially promising, is neither environmentally-friendly nor reliable. A future adoption of **nuclear fusion** power plants has the potential to solve humanity's **desire** for an unlimited supply of clean, sustainable and reliable electricity, but the **harsh reality** is that the Earth does not have the resources to feed and shelter 8+ billion humans in a sustainable way. The **wants** of too many polluting people chasing an elusive dollar is not sustainable. Some people may **want** to save the elephants. Many **want** to protect our wildlife. Rescue shelters **want** to save our dogs and cats. But who **wants** to save humans from themselves. **THIS IS THE HARSH REALITY**.

I would like to thank the readers of this book who have spent the time and effort to educate themselves about the **harsh reality** of global warming. You now know more about this subject than most.

Citations

Chapter 1

[1] Kuipers, Dean, November 18, 2011. Greenhouse gases, water vapor and you. *Los Angeles Times.* Retrieved from https://globalchange.mit.edu/news-media/in-the-news/greenhouse-gases-water-vapor-and-you

[2] World Population: 1950-2050. Retrieved from https://www.census.gov/library/visualizations/2011/demo/world-population--1950-2050.html

[3] Retrieved from https://en.wikipedia.org/wiki/Chlorofluorocarbon

Chapter 2

[4] Hedges, John, June 24, 2021. How many cars are there in the world in 2022? *Hedges & Company.* Retrieved from https://hedgescompany.com/blog/2021/06/how-many-cars-are-there-in-the-world/

[5] Ritchie, Hannah, October 6, 2020. Cars, planes, trains: Where do CO^2 emissions from transport come from? Retrieved from https://ourworldindata.org/co2-emissions-from-transport

[6] https://en.wikipedia.org/wiki/Henry_Ford

[7] Ibid

[8] Ibid

Chapter 3

[9] Author Unknown, May 2021. Carbon Dioxide Emissions From Electricity. Retrieved from https://world-nuclear.org/information-library/energy-and-the-environment/co2-implications-of-electricity-generation.aspx

[10] https://en.wikipedia.org/wiki/Faraday%27s_law_of_induction

[11] https://en.wikipedia.org/wiki/Michael_Faraday

[12] Giancoli, Douglas C. (2008). *Physics for Scientists and Engineers.* Pearson Education Inc.

[13] https://en.wikipedia.org/wiki/James_Clerk_Maxwell

Chapter 4

[14] https://en.wikipedia.org/wiki/Nikola_Tesla

[15] https://en.wikipedia.org/wiki/Thomas_Edison

Chapter 5

[16] https://en.wikipedia.org/wiki/Fritz_Haber

[17] https://en.wikipedia.org/wiki/Carl_Bosch

Chapter 6

[18] Gilmore, Paul, May 4, 2022. How Much Carbon Dioxide Does A Tree Absorb Per Year? (Solution) Retrieved from https://www.klriver.org/faq/how-much-carbon-dioxide-does-a-tree-absorb-per-year-solution.html

[19] https://en.wikipedia.org/wiki/Direct_air_capture

[20] Ibid

[21] Ibid

[22] Ibid

[23] Ibid

[24] Retrieved from https://mechanicaltrees.com/mechanicaltrees/

[25] https://www.arpa-e.energy.gov/technologies/exploratory-topics/direct-ocean-capture

Chapter 7

[26] Dorger, Samantha, October 19, 2022. Foods of the Future that Could Change the World. *The Street.* Retrieved from https://www.thestreet.com/personal-finance/foods-of-future-that-could-change-world#gid=ci02aa23dd400026ce&pid=3d-printed-food-sh

[27] Ibid

[28] Ibid

[29] Whyte, L. E. (2022, November 17). Lab-Grown Poultry Clears Its First Hurdle at the FDA. *The Wall Street Journal.*

[30] Dorger, Samantha, October 19, 2022. Foods of the Future that Could Change the World. *The Street.* Retrieved from https://www.thestreet.com/personal-finance/foods-of-future-that-could-change-world#gid=ci02aa23dd400026ce&pid=3d-printed-food-sh

[31] Ibid

[32] Ibid

[33] Lounsbrough, Craig D., Retrieved from https://craiglpc.com/author/

[34] Retrieved from https://www.ncei.noaa.gov/products/paleoclimatology/paleo-perspectives/global-warming

Chapter 8

[35] Buis, Alan, NASA"s Jet Propulsion Laboratory, February 27, 2020. Milankovitch Orbital Cycles and their Role in Earth's Climate. Retrieved from https://climate.nasa.gov/news/2948/milankovitch-orbital-cycles-and-their-role-in-earths-climate/

[36] https://en.wikipedia.org/wiki/Milutin_Milankovi%C4%87

[37] Retrieved from https://www.ncei.noaa.gov/news/how-can-ice-teach-us-about-climate

[38] Retrieved from https://icecores.org/about-ice-cores

[39] Retrieved from https://gml.noaa.gov/ccgg/trends/

[40] Susmita Dasgupta, Somik V. Lall and David Wheeler, (November 17, 2021). Deploying 'sentinel satellites' to monitor greenhouse gas emissions. *Brookings*. https://www.brookings.edu/blog/future-development/2021/11/17/deploying-sentinel-satellites-to-monitor-greenhouse-gas-emissions/

[41] Rebecca Lindsay and Luann Dahlman, (August 17, 2020). Climate Change: Ocean Heat Content. *NOAA Climate.gov* Retrieved from https://www.climate.gov/news-features/understanding-climate/climate-change-ocean-heat-content

[42] Ibid

[43] Ibid

[44] Retrieved https://www.fisheries.noaa.gov/insight/understanding-ocean-acidification

[45] Retrieved from https://ocean.si.edu/ocean-life/invertebrates/ocean-acidification

Chapter 9

[46] Glacier National Park in pictures – the author's private collection

Chapter 10

[47] Retrieved from https://en.wikipedia.org/wiki/Steven_E._Koonin#Publications

[48] Koonin, Steven E. (2021). *Unsettled*. BebBella Books, Inc., Dallas, TX.

[49] IPCC, 2021: Summary for Policymakers. In: *Climate Change 2021: The Physical Science Basis. Contribution of Working Group I to the 6th Assessment Report of the Intergovernmental Panel on Climate Change* [Masson-Delmotte, V., P. Zhai, A. Pirani, S. L. Connors, C Pean, S. Berger, N. Caud, Y. Chen, L. Goldfarb, M. I. Gomis, M. Huang, K. Leitzell, E. Lonnoy, J. B. R. Matthews, T. K. Maycock, T. Waterfield, O. Yelekci, R. Yu, and B. Zhou (eds.)]. In Press

[50] Ibid

[51] Ibid

[52] Toomey, Diane. (July 2, 2014). Where Will Earth Head After Its 'Climate Departure'? *Yale Environment 360* Retrieved from https://e360.yale.edu/features/interview_camilo_mora_where_will_earth_head_after_its_climate_departure

[53] Hersher, Rebecca, Rott, Nathan, Sommer, Lauren. (August 28, 2020). Everything is Unprecedented: Welcome to Your Hotter Earth. *NPR.*

[54] Retrieved from https://www.azquotes.com/author/4399-Albert_Einstein

[55] Retrieved from https://en.wikipedia.org/wiki/Enrico_Fermi

[56] Retrieved from https://www.livescience.com/fermi-paradox

[57] Retrieved from https://interestingengineering.com/culture/the-15-most-ridiculous-and-ridiculously-amazing-elon-musk-quotes

[58] Retrieved from https://www.brainyquote.com/authors/stephen-hawking-quotes

Chapter 11

[59] Baker, Aryn. (September 12, 2019). What It's Like Living in One of the Hottest Cities on Earth – Where It May Soon be Uninhabitable. *Time.*

[60] Retrieved from https://en.wikipedia.org/wiki/Australian_Open_extreme_heat_policy

[61] Renwick, James. (September 17, 2017). Climate Explained: why we won't be heading into an ice age anytime soon. *The Conversation.* Retrieved from https://theconversation.com/climate-explained-why-we-wont-be-heading-into-an-ice-age-any-time-soon-123675

[62] Buis, Alan. (February 27, 2020). Why Milankovitch (Obital Cycles) Can't Explain Earth's Current Warming. *NASA*. Retrieved from https://climate.nasa.gov/ask-nasa-climate/2949/why-milankovitch-orbital-cycles-cant-explain-earths-current-warming/

[63] Larson, Nina. (May 3, 2023). World should prepare for El Nino. New record temperatures. *Agence France-Presse (AFP)*. Retrieved from https://www.france24.com/en/live-news/20230503-world-should-prepare-for-el-nino-new-record-temperatures-un

[64] Hood, Marlowe. (June 6, 2023). Artic could be ice-free a decade earlier than thought. *Agence France-Presse (AFP)*. Retrieved from https://www.yahoo.com/news/arctic-could-ice-free-decade-002528215.html

Chapter 12

[65] Cooper, Michael. (September 26, 2014). Defining Problem: The Most Important Business Skill You've Never Been Taught. *NBCNews*. Retrieved from https://www.nbcnews.com/id/wbna56125046

[66] Mendoza, Jim. (March 31, 2021). To create a carbon neutral Hawaii, this UH professor is working to plant 1M trees this year. *Hawaii News Now*. Retrieved from https://www.hawaiinewsnow.com/2021/04/01/create-carbon-neutral-hawaii-this-uh-professor-is-working-plant-m-trees-year/

[67] Moseman, Andrew. (June 16, 2022). How many new trees would we need to offset our carbon emissions? *MIT Climate*. Retrieved from https://climate.mit.edu/ask-mit/how-many-new-trees-would-we-need-offset-our-carbon-emissions

[68] Lai, Olivia. (November 2, 2022). 10 Amazon Rainforest Deforestation Facts to Know About. *Earth.org*. Retrieved from https://earth.org/amazon-rainforest-deforestation-facts/

[69] Ibid

[70] Retrieved from https://en.wikipedia.org/wiki/Nile

[71] Hannah Ritchie, Max Roser and Pablo Rosado (2022) – "Energy". Published online at OurWorldInData.org. Retrieved from https://ourworldindata.org/energy [online resource]

[71] Retrieved from https://en.wikipedia.org/wiki/Three_Gorges_Dam

[72] Retrieved from https://en.wikipedia.org/wiki/Baihetan_Dam

[73] Retrieved from https://www.statista.com/statistics/271748/the-largest-emitters-of-co2-in-the-world/

[74] Jennifer Hiller and William Boston, (December 14, 2022). Breakthrough Heats Up Fusion Sector. *Wall Street Journal*.

[75] Hiller, Jennifer, (April 24, 2023). Tech Billionaires Bet on Fusion To Deliver Energy. *Wall Street Journal*.

[76] Ibid

[77] Hiller, Jennifer, (May 11, 2023). Software Giant Strikes Fusion Deal In Gamble on Unproven Power Tech. *Wall Street Journal*.

[78] Ibid

[79] Retrieved from https://www.researchgate.net/figure/World-Population-Growth-1950-2050-41_fig1_325002825

[80] Retrieved from https://www.theworldcounts.com/challenges/planet-earth/state-of-the-planet/world-population-clock-live

[81] Christensen, Jen. (August 30, 2022). Elon Musk thinks the population will collapse. Demographers say it's not happening. *CNN*. Retrieved from https://www.cnn.com/2022/08/30/health/elon-musk-population-collapse-wellness/index.html

[82] Solon, Olivia. (March 11, 2018). Elon Musk: we must colonize Mars to preserve our species in a third world war. *The Guardian*. Retrieved from https://www.theguardian.com/technology/2018/mar/11/elon-musk-colonise-mars-third-world-war

Photo Credits

p 3 – Lake Mead

p 4 – Glacier National Park

p 13 – Henry Ford

p 18 – Michael Faraday

p 23 – Nickola Tesla

p 24 – Thomas Edison

p 28 – Mina Miller Edison

p 31 – Fritz Haber

p 33 – Clara Immerwahr

p 34 – Carl Bosch

p 47 – Deep-fried insects sold in Bangkok

p 48 – Chief Theodore holding white fonio in Senegal

p 80 – Mt. Jackson

p 81 – Mt. St. Nicholas

p 82 – Jackson Glacier

p 83 – Lake McDonald

p 84 – Flathead Lake

p 91 – Steven E, Koonin

p 100 – Camilo Mora

p 102 – Albert Einstein

p 104 – Enrico Fermi

p 105 – Elon Musk

p 106 – Stephen Hawking

Glossary

AI – Artificial Intelligence

Amazon – A Large tropical rainforest occupying the drainage basin of the Amazon River located in northern South America and covering an area of 2.3 million square miles. The Amazon occupies about 40% of Brazil's total area.

Afforestation – refers to the planting of trees in an area where trees have not been recently cut down.

Anomalies – something that deviates from the standard, normal or what is expected.

AR6 – 6th Assessment Report of the IPCC

CO_2 – carbon dioxide is a chemical compound consisting of one carbon atom and two oxygen atoms

Cover crops – plants that cover soil and act to manage soil erosion, soil fertility and soil quality.

DAC – direct air capture

Deforestation – The removal of trees from forests or other lands on a large scale for the benefit of human activities.

$E = mc^2$ – mass and energy are two different forms of the same thing.

Eccentricity – the eccentricity or an elliptical orbit is the measure of its deviation from a circle.

Equilibrium – refers to a balance of forces; it can be mechanical, thermal or chemical.

La Nina – refers to the periodic cooling of sea-surface temperatures across the east-central equatorial Pacific. It represents the **cold** phase of the El Nino Southern Oscillation (ENSO).

El Nino – refers to the above average sea-surface temperatures that periodically develop across the east-central equatorial Pacific. It represents the **warm** phase of the El Nino Southern Oscillation (ENSO).

Forest – Areas having at least 50% tree cover.

Nuclear Fission – the release of energy from splitting the nucleus of a heavy atom (e. g. uranium $_{235}$) into two or more smaller nuclei.

Nuclear Fusion – the release of energy from the combining of light elements (e. g. fusing two hydrogen nuclei into helium).

GERD – Great Ethiopian Renaissance Dam

GW – Gigawatt (one billion watts)

Gastronomy – the art or science of good eating. Gastronomy is also the study of the relationship between food and culture, the art of preparing appetizing food, utilizing the cooking styles of various regions.

General Theory of Relativity – applies to non-inertial reference frames where the laws of physics are different (e. g. accelerating reference frames).

Ghee – a clarified butter that results from separating milk solids and butterfat in processed butter.

GHG – Greenhouse gas

In situ – Latin for onsite or in position (stationary)

IPCC – Intergovernmental Panel on Climate Change

Hydroxyl bond in water vapor – formed when two hydrogen atoms bond with an oxygen atom (e. g. H_2O) producing a dipolar molecule that strongly absorbs electromagnetic radiation in the infrared spectrum.

Joule – unit of energy in SI units

Kigali Amendment – an amendment to the Montreal Protocol that will phase out the production and use of HFCs.

Le Chatelier's Principle – states that if a dynamic equilibrium is disturbed by changing the conditions, the position of equilibrium shifts to counteract the change.

MW – Megawatt (one million watts)

Maize – A cereal grain first domesticated by indigenous people of Southern Mexico approximately 10,000 years ago.

Mechanical Tree – artificial tree 10 meters high consisting of tiles that passively absorb CO_2

Megawatts – A unit of power and equal to one million watts of electricity.

Obliquity – angle between the plane of the Earth's orbit and the celestial equator.

Ozone layer – a layer in the Earth's stratosphere containing a high concentration of O_3 which absorbs most of UV radiation coming from the Sun.

Permeability of free space (μ_0) – constant that measures the ability of magnetic fields to pass through a vacuum.

Permittivity of free space (ε_0) – constant that measures the ability of electric fields to pass through a vacuum.

Paleoclimate – ancient climate

Paleoclimatology data – derived from natural sources such as tree rings, ice cores, corals, stalagmites and ocean and lake sediments.

Precession – a change in the orientation of the Earth's rotational axis.

Proxies – imprints used to reconstruct past climates. Examples of imprints include organisms, like diatoms, forams, coral, tree rings and ice cores

Quantum Mechanics – theory that describes the physical properties of atoms and subatomic particles (the very small).

Ton – imperial unit of **weight** = 2,240 lbs.

Tonne – metric unit of **mass** = 1000 kg (1000 kg exerts 2204.6 lbs of force at sea level)

Inertia Reference Frame – where the laws of physics have the same form.

Red Tide – name given to the algae species **Karenia brevis,** which is a dinoflagellate that will color the ocean a deep red.

Reforestation – refers to the replanting of trees on land that has previously had trees, but where these trees were recently cut down.

Second Law of Thermodynamics – heat always moves from hotter objects to colder objects.

SI units – the international system of units (based on metric system)

Special Theory of Relativity – Albert Einstein used two postulates to explain his theory. 1. The laws of physics have the same form in all inertial reference frames. 2. The speed of light is a constant in free space, independent of the speed of the observer or the source.

Specific heat – amount of heat energy required to raise the temperature of a body per unit mass (e.g. water; 4.18 joules; air; 1.0035 joules (J)

Spinout – the outcome of independent decisions of employees that leave the parent firm to start a new venture.

Strawman argument – a flawed line of reasoning that substitutes an opposing argument with a distorted or misrepresented version of it in order to make it easier to defeat.

Superconducting Magnet – is an electromagnet made from coils of superconducting wire.

Superconducting Wire – wire that has zero resistance, which allow for larger currents that normal wire.

Umami – a taste in food (other than sweet, sour, salt and bitter) similar to the taste of glutamates.

Ultraviolet radiation (UV) – electromagnetic radiation, having a wavelength shorter than visible light and longer than x-rays and gamma rays.

Vegetative method – an asexual method of plant reproduction that occurs in its leaves, roots and stem.

Wet Bulb Temperature – The lowest temperature to which air can be cooled by the evaporation of water into the air at constant pressure.

WGI – Working Group I

Printed in Great Britain
by Amazon